D1413256

Extraordinary Jobs in

AGRICULTURE
AND NATURE

Also in the Extraordinary Jobs series:

Extraordinary Jobs for Adventurers
Extraordinary Jobs with Animals
Extraordinary Jobs for Creative People
Extraordinary Jobs in Entertainment
Extraordinary Jobs in the Food Industry
Extraordinary Jobs in Government
Extraordinary Jobs in Health and Science
Extraordinary Jobs in Leisure
Extraordinary Jobs in Media
Extraordinary Jobs in the Service Sector
Extraordinary Jobs in Sports

Extraordinary Jobs in

AGRICULTURE AND NATURE

ALECIA T. DEVANTIER & CAROL A. TURKINGTON

Ferguson

An imprint of Infobase Publishing

Extraordinary Jobs in Agriculture and Nature

Ferguson
An imprint of Infobase Publishing
132 West 31st Street
New York NY 10001

Library of Congress Cataloging-in-Publication Data
Devantier, Alecia T.
  Extraordinary jobs in agriculture and nature / Alecia T. Devantier and Carol A. Turkington.
    p. cm. — (Extraordinary jobs in nature)
  Includes bibliographical references and index.
  ISBN 0-8160-5854-7 (hc : alk. paper)
  1. Agriculture—Vocational guidance—United States. 2. Forests and forestry—Vocational guidance—United States. 3. Outdoor life—Vocational guidance—United States. I. Turkington, Carol. II. Title. III. Series
  S494.5.A4D48 2006
  630'.2'0373—dc22   2005019880

Ferguson books are available at special discounts when purchased in bulk quantities for businesses, associations, institutions, or sales promotions. Please call our Special Sales Department in New York at (212) 967-8800 or (800) 322-8755.

You can find Ferguson on the World Wide Web at http://www.fergpubco.com

Text design by Mary Susan Ryan-Flynn
Cover design by Salvatore Luongo

Printed in the United States of America

VB KT 10 9 8 7 6 5 4 3 2 1

This book is printed on acid-free paper.

CONTENTS

Acknowledgments vii
Are You Cut Out for a Career
    in Agriculture or Nature? ix
How to Use This Book xi

Agronomist 1
Alpaca Farmer 5
Beekeeper 9
Buffalo Herder 13
Bug Wrangler 17
Christmas Tree Grower 21
Citrus Grower 25
Crab Fisherman 28
Cranberry Farmer 32
Crop Duster 36
Deer Farmer 39
Dowser 43
Emu Farmer 46
Fish Farmer 50
Forestry Consultant 53
Game Bird Producer
    and Hunt Organizer 57
Game Warden 60

Hiking Trail Designer 64
Insect Control Technician 67
Irrigation Specialist 71
Landscape Designer 74
Maple Syrup Producer 77
Mushroom Grower 80
Orchard Operator 83
Organic Farm Manager 86
Oyster Shucker 90
Park Ranger 93
Peanut Farmer 97
Range Manager 100
Timber Harvester 103
Topiary Gardener 107
Turf Scientist 111
Winegrower (Viticulturist) 114

Appendix A. Associations,
    Organizations, and Web Sites . . 118
Appendix B. Online Career
    Resources 131
Appendix C. Agricultural Colleges
    and Universities 139
Read More About It 146
Index 155

ACKNOWLEDGMENTS

We would like to thank Susan Shelly McGovern, Barbara Turkington, Elaine Bernarding, and the staffs at Walt Disney, Penn State, the Denver Broncos, the Potomac River Fisheries Commission, Cape Cod Cranberry Growers' Association, the American Emu Association, the National Peanut Board, and the Sports Turf Managers Association. We'd also like to gratefully acknowledge the unceasing efforts of our editors at Infobase Publishing, Sarah Fogarty and James Chambers, as well as Infobase Publishing staffer Vanessa Nittoli, and our agents Ed Claflin and Gene Brissie.

ARE YOU CUT OUT FOR A CAREER IN AGRICULTURE OR NATURE?

Imagine this scenario: It's a few years into the future, and you're sitting in your cubicle, half-hidden by a drifting mass of items paperclipped together. The boss sticks her head around your partition and wants to know when the Harbinger Report will be finished. And while you're at it, can you stay late to tie up the loose ends with the Farquar situation?

You stare out the window. (If you're lucky, you get a window, and if you're really lucky, you might be able to crane your neck to catch a glimpse of the park). You sit watching two squirrels play hide-and-seek, until you hear the boss making her way back to your office. Time to flip open that report and pretend to be interested.

Are your toes curling up at the thought? Would you rather plant an acre of Vidalia onions than print out one more report? Would you rather use your hands to reel in a crab line on the Chesapeake than fix widgets on an assembly line? Do you dream of striding across the plains, checking the health of forests and grasslands, or are you solely focused on toting up the year-end profit-and-loss statement so you get your Christmas bonus on time this year?

Let's face it: Some people are made for working in the great outdoors. They're made for wearing rubber waders and a slicker, not a Burberry's tweed suit, and they'll never fit inside a normal 9-to-5 time slot.

And that's okay.

Take some time to think about the kind of person you are, and the sorts of experiences you dream of having. Ask yourself: Is there something I'd rather be doing for the rest of my life that would make me truly happy? Am I passionate about something?

If you want a career in the open, you'd better be passionate, because if it's lots of money you're looking for, well, many of these back-to-the-land jobs don't pay that much. What they do offer, however, is something much harder to measure—an experience that will let your spirit soar and allows you to do what you love to do.

Of course, loving what you do is only part of having a successful career in nature and agriculture. You've got to be willing to work hard. Too many times, kids have the idea that they'll graduate into a world just dying to give them a job.

It may not always be easy. Can you imagine what Luther Burbank's mother said when he told her he wanted to sit out in the shed and work with seeds? What George Washington Carver's father might have thought when he heard his son wanted to dedicate his life to figuring out things to do with peanuts?

Of course, a lucky few of you will have been born into this farm or forest lifestyle, and your path may be clear to you. But the rest of you may just have inherited a lot of "shoulds" in thinking about the kind of person you want to be. These *shoulds* inside your head can be a major stumbling block in finding and enjoying an unusual career in agriculture or nature. Everybody knows about the typical jobs that are out there. We wrote this book to help you see the world of atypical careers you may never have thought about—jobs you may not even have known existed, or that you didn't realize would actually pay a salary. Remember, if you're born with a dream, you owe it to yourself to go after it, no matter how unusual or just plain batty it may seem to others. Don't cheat yourself. Like everyone, you're going to get older, so you might as well get older doing what you love to do. What you need to do.

You'll also need to realize that there may be other people who aren't so happy with your career choice. You may hear complaints from your family and friends who just can't understand why you don't want a "regular" job. Some people think working outdoors only qualifies as a hobby ("Surely you don't intend to make a living growing mushrooms!"). If you confide your career dreams to others, you may find they try to discourage you. Can you handle their continuous skepticism?

What's become clear as we researched this book is that a career in nature or agriculture is usually more than a job—it's a way of looking at life with reverence and respect, of trying to protect what's left in the natural world before it disappears forever. We've encountered sad stories of a disappearing lifestyle in this country, of shrinking family farms and the difficulty the "little guy" faces in making a living competing with giant agribusinesses. But there are also heartening stories of niche farms and specialty careers popping up from Maine to New Mexico. Living a natural lifestyle is all about learning to look at the world through curious eyes. Being so close to nature, you're attuned to life at its most basic.

There are still a lot of misconceptions about working in nature and agriculture. Lots of people think of a person working in agriculture as somebody who scratches a modest living from a few acres of land or a couple of animals. Others think of "nature jobs" as volunteer-type positions for sandal-wearing hippies who want to hug trees. In reality, there are so many unusual careers available in agriculture and nature that it's mind-boggling.

Want to work outside? Consider becoming a cranberry farmer, an emu oil producer, or a landscape professional. Want to contribute to the industry a different way? Study agriculture research, sales, or marketing. Or you could become a feed manufacturer, lab technician, zookeeper, rangelands management consultant, or agricultural education teacher!

Interested in earth science? You can work out in the field or in a lab as a turf or soil scientist or agronomist. People needed in this area include soil nutrient management specialists, crop production consultants, and environmental management professionals. Soil scientists study erosion, soil makeup, and the movement of water and toxins through soil.

Are you interested in pursuing business? Combine agriculture and business with an agribusiness major and become an agricultural entrepreneur. If you're a sports fan, consider studying turf grass science and be responsible for keeping golf courses lush, football fields playable, and lawns manicured. Or you could try a career in conservation, topiary, or horticulture.

Living and working close to nature isn't necessarily an easy career. You'll work hard—very hard. But if you allow yourself to explore the options that are out there, you'll find that work and play often tend to become the same thing. So push past your doubts and fears—and let your journey begin!

Carol A. Turkington
Alecia T. Devantier

HOW TO USE THIS BOOK

Students face a lot of pressure to decide what they want to be when they grow up. For some students, the decision is easy, but for others, the choice isn't nearly so clear. If you're not interested in a traditional, indoor 9-to-5 job—if you feel the need to have the sun shining in your face and the wind blowing at your back—you're probably looking for a unique way to make a living. And you're probably wondering where you can go to get answers to your questions about these exciting, nontraditional jobs.

Where can you go to find out how to become an alpaca farmer? Do you have what it takes to become a park ranger or a range manager? Where do you learn how to be the manager of an organic farm? Is it really possible to make a living as a hiking trail designer? Where would you go for training if you wanted to be a turf scientist or a mushroom grower? What's the job outlook for an irrigation specialist?

Look no further! This book will take you inside the world of a number of different occupations in the field of agriculture, answering your questions, letting you know what to expect if you pursue that career, introducing you to someone making a living that way, and providing resources if you want to do further research.

THE JOB PROFILES

All job profiles in this book have been broken down into the following fact-filled sections: At a Glance, Overview, and Interview. Each offers a distinct perspective on the job, and taken together give you a full view of the job in question.

At a Glance

Each profile starts out with an At a Glance box, offering a snapshot of important basic information to give you a quick glimpse of that particular job, including salary, education/experience, personal attributes, requirements, and outlook.

- *Salary range.* What can you expect to make? Salary ranges for the jobs in this book are as accurate as possible; many are based on data from the U.S. Bureau of Labor Statistics' *Occupational Outlook Handbook.* Information also comes from individuals, actual job ads, employers, and experts in that field. It's important to remember that, especially in the agriculture industry, salaries for any particular job vary greatly depending on factors such as location, product demand, and the size of your operation. Profit and loss are also subject to factors beyond your control, such as drought or excessive rain, heat, insects, and so forth.

- *Education/Experience.* What kind of education or experience does the job require? This section will give you some information about the types of education requirements agriculture and nature jobs might have. While agriculture jobs used to be mostly learned by doing or passed along within families, modern agriculture has become a highly sophisticated, scientific field, requiring both skills and knowledge in science and business.

✅ *Personal attributes.* Do you have what it takes to do this job? How do you think of yourself? How would someone else describe you? This section will give you an idea of some of the personality characteristics and traits that might be useful to you if you choose this career. These attributes were collected from articles written about the job, as well as recommendations from employers and people actually doing the jobs, working in the field.

✅ *Requirements.* Are you qualified? Jobs in agriculture often require the ability to perform hard physical work; to operate large, sophisticated equipment; and to be able to market your product and keep up with complicated business procedures. You might as well make sure you meet any health, medical, or screening requirements before going any further with your job pursuit.

✅ *Outlook.* What are your chances of finding a job? This section is based in part on the *Occupational Outlook Handbook*, as well as interviews with employers and experts doing the jobs. This information is typically a best guess based on the information that is available right now, including changes in the economy, situations in the country, and job trends, as well as many other factors that can influence changes in the availability of jobs.

Overview

This section will give you an idea of what to expect from the job. For most of these jobs, there really is no such thing as an average day. Each new day, new job, or new assignment is a whole new adventure, bringing with it a unique set of challenges and rewards. This section provides an overview of what a person holding this position might expect on a day-to-day basis.

This section also gives more details about how to get into the profession. It takes a more detailed look at the required training or education, if needed, giving an in-depth look at what to expect during that training or educational period. If there are no training or education requirements for the job, this section will provide some suggestions for getting the experience you'll need to be successful.

No job is perfect, and the **Pitfalls** section takes a look at some of the obvious and not-so-obvious pitfalls of the job. Don't let the pitfalls discourage you from pursuing the career; they are just things to be aware of while making your decision.

For many people, loving their job so much that they look forward to going to work every day is enough of a perk. The **Perks** section will look at some of the other perks of the job you may not have considered.

What can you do now to start working toward the career of your dreams? **Get a Jump on the Job** will give you some ideas and suggestions for things that you can do now, even before graduating, to start preparing for this job. Opportunities include courses you can take now in high school that will help you later; training programs, groups, and organizations to join; as well as practical skills to learn.

Interview

In addition to taking a general look at the job, each entry features a discussion with someone who is lucky enough to do this job for a living. In addition to giving you an inside look at the job, the experts offer advice for people wanting to follow in their footsteps, pursuing a career in the same field.

APPENDIXES

Appendix A (Associations, Organizations, and Web Sites) lists places to look for additional information about each specific job, including professional associations and helpful Web sites. Associations are a great source of information, and there's an association for just about everything. If there is an association for the job or career in this book, we've listed it here. Many associations have a student membership level which you can join by paying a small fee. There are many advantages to joining an association, including the chance to make important contacts, receive helpful newsletters, and attend workshops or conferences. Some associations also offer scholarships that will make it easier to further your education. Other sources listed in this section include information about accredited training programs, forums, and more.

In **Appendix B (Online Career Resources)** we've gathered some of the best general Web sites about unusual jobs in agriculture and nature. Use these as a springboard to your own Internet research. All of this information was current as of the writing of this book, but Web site addresses do change. If you can't find what you're looking for at a given address, do a simple Web search. The page may have been moved to a different location.

Lastly, if it's agriculture you're interested in, **Appendix C (Agricultural Colleges and Universities)** lists some of the best colleges with related courses and degree programs.

READ MORE ABOUT IT

In this back-of-the-book listing, we've gathered some helpful books that can give you more detailed information about a particular job. Find these at the library or bookstore if you want to learn even more about jobs in agriculture and nature.

AGRONOMIST

OVERVIEW

Have you eaten a fresh-picked tomato from a garden stand by the side of the road? Watched a farmer tilling the soil? If you get a job as an agronomist, it could be your responsibility to make sure the food everybody eats is healthy, and that farmers are using the best methods to grow these crops. This is all part of the job of an agronomist—also known as agriculture and food scientists.

While the basic definition sounds simple, the number of jobs and types of employers varies widely for agronomists. These specialists work on improving agriculture productivity and the safety of the food supply, studying soil and food production, and figuring out how to develop methods to conserve and manage soil, in addition to rehabilitating damaged or polluted land. Agronomists study farm crops and animals, manage research programs, and try to improve crop yields. They are also instrumental in developing safe management of pests and weeds and conservation of land, soil, and water.

As an agronomist, you might be found teaching, conducting business, and doing research in universities, food production, and environmental industries around the world. You could work as a freelance consultant or work for the government in a variety of its agriculture programs; in fact, almost half of salaried agronomists work for the federal, state, or local governments, including the U.S. Department of Agriculture, state Departments of Agriculture, the Soil Conservation Service,

AT A GLANCE

Salary Range

Salaries vary widely depending on area, degree (bachelor's through Ph.D.), and employer, but may range from $28,750 to more than $85,460. The average federal salary for employees in non-supervisory, supervisory, and managerial positions in agronomy is $68,846.

Education/Experience

A bachelor's degree in agricultural science is required; for any type of research, a master's or a doctorate is required. A Ph.D. also is typically required to be a college professor. In addition, degrees in other fields can be applied to an agronomy career (such as degrees in biology, chemistry, physics, and some engineering specialties). Courses should include communications, business, life sciences, economics, agricultural science courses, as well as broad-based general education courses, including English and speech.

Personal Attributes

Should have an interest in science and environmental issues and enjoy working with people, in addition to being able to work both independently and in teams. Should also have a keen interest in applying science to practical feed and food production issues, good oral and written communication skills, with a good understanding of business principles. Computer skills are a must; basic research skills also are helpful.

Requirements

Agronomists can become certified in several fields including crops, agronomy, crop advising, soils, horticulture, plant pathology, and weed science. The American Society of Agronomy offers certification programs for agronomists who have passed designated examinations and have at least two years of experience with at least a bachelor's degree in agriculture (or four years of experience with no degree).

(continues)

AT A GLANCE (continued)

Outlook

Jobs are expected to grow more slowly than average, according to government estimates, but employment is relatively stable during periods of economic recession. Layoffs are less likely among agricultural scientists than in some other occupations because food is a staple item and its demand fluctuates very little with economic activity.

and as agriculturists in foreign countries. Others work for companies that produce food products or agricultural supplies, such as seed, agricultural supply, and lawn-care companies; or for farming-related companies such as banks or farm co-ops. Soils specialists conduct all types of research in soil and water management and land use.

Agronomists also research ways to produce crops and turf, and ways to manage soils in the most environmentally friendly way. And lest you think it's all just farms—agronomists also may work as weather forecasters, environmentalists, researchers, or teachers.

Armed with a bachelor's degree in agronomy, you may work as a manager in businesses dealing with ranchers and farmers, such as feed, fertilizer, seed, and farm equipment manufacturers; retailers or wholesalers; and farm credit institutions. In some cases, persons with a four-year

Heather Karston, agronomist

It seems that ecology and nature were always a passion for agronomist Heather Karston, Ph.D., now a Penn State University associate professor of crop and soil sciences. A professor and agroecology researcher, Karston studies pasture plant ecology, grazing system management, cropping systems, crop rotations, and soil management. Basically, this means she wants to make the world a healthier place for humans, plants, and wildlife.

Passionate about ecology, she started out earning a bachelor's degree in environmental biology, but soon began to realize the importance that agricultural practices played in the environment. In other words, the methods a farmer chose to use in the fields could directly affect the soil, water, and forests in the surrounding countryside. "As an undergraduate, I realized that agriculture is a major part of our environmental resources," she explains, "and will need to continue to be. For me, agroecology is important in maintaining a healthy food system protecting human health as well as water and air."

Realizing that the link between agriculture and ecology would play an important part in the future, she recognized that this was a field that would continue to provide necessary jobs. As a result, she went on to earn a master's and Ph.D. in agronomy. As a researcher and teacher, her job is to apply the sciences of plant physiology and soil chemistry, along with general soil science and pest management. She's particularly interested in figuring out how to design more ecologically sustainable agricultural systems, she explains. Her research and teaching explores how to reduce nutrient loss and what practices can reduce the need for pesticides. She's

degree can provide consulting services, or become a certified crop advisor, providing crop management recommendations to farmers to help them meet their objectives. Bachelor's degree holders also can work in some applied research and product development positions, but usually only in certain subfields, such as food science and technology, and the federal government hires bachelor's degree holders to work as soil scientists. Four-year degrees also may help you as a farmer or ranch manager, cooperative extension service agent, agricultural products inspector, or purchasing or sales agent for agricultural commodity or farm supply companies.

Most of the time, agronomists specialize in one area. One agronomist may try to figure out how to grow plants organically, working with organic farmers to improve their techniques. Research agronomists may toil in laboratories run by the government or private industries, experimenting with new chemical pesticides and herbicides. Still others focus on the plants themselves, trying to manipulate the plant's genes to create new, stronger species that can better fight off disease or pests. Some prefer a more educational role, working one on one with farmers to improve production.

Pitfalls

The field of agronomy is not without controversy; some agronomists are health-

interested in anything that might reduce the world's dependency on fossil fuels, and that would protect water quality and wildlife habitat.

She was also attracted to agronomy because of her interest in international studies. "There are lots of opportunities to study agriculture in other countries and to learn from people in other countries," she says. Karston studied in New Zealand for a year for her Ph.D., because of the importance of grazing systems as the basis of agriculture in that country. She also studied international agriculture, spending time in Honduras, studying Spanish in Guatemala, and as a teaching assistant in Costa Rica for tropical agroecological systems.

"One of the things I really enjoy is really being outdoors and working with plants and animals and insects, as well as with the people who are farming or consuming the products," she says. "I think mostly I really enjoy plants and the outdoors." The challenge, she notes, is that as a university professor, she spends a lot of time analyzing data, writing grants, and grading papers. "I don't enjoy the paperwork," she admits, "and the bureaucracy involved in reporting data. I don't really enjoy the time spent writing grants that don't always get funded."

She does enjoy her time spent in the classroom teaching, however. "That's what's great about being an academic agronomist," she says. "And I do enjoy doing research. That's one of the reasons to choose an academic position—if you like studying and learning new things, research is a great way to do that."

oriented scientists trying to figure out how to increase the world's food supply without using pesticides or chemicals, while other agronomists advocate genetic enhancement and chemical modification.

Perks

For people who truly love agriculture or ecology, who enjoy working with farms and food producers, or who are interested in preserving nature and wildlife and conserving natural resources, the agronomy track can be a fulfilling career.

Get a Jump on the Job

To prepare for this career, in high school you should take a variety of college prep courses including biology, chemistry, physics, and mathematics; English, speech, and foreign languages will strengthen communication skills. The government is a great resource for finding more information about jobs in agronomy. You can use the Internet to find other sites about agronomy. Some organizations to check out include the American Society of Agronomy, Food and Agricultural Center for Tomorrow, and the Institute for Food Technologists.

Experience also can help; one good way to get started on this career path is to find a position as a summer student with an agricultural board, or even summer work on a farm or ranch.

ALPACA FARMER

OVERVIEW

Why would you consider raising cows or pigs when there are cute, gentle alpacas to be had? Alpacas originated in the Andes Mountains, where they were revered by the Incan civilization. First imported to the United States in 1984, alpacas are becoming increasingly popular in this country, and for good reasons. Soft and furry, with big eyes and long eyelashes, alpacas are generally easy to raise—and they live for a long time by animal standards (the average life span is 20 years), which is beneficial for breeding purposes.

They don't bite, butt, or claw, largely due to the fact that they have no incisors, hooves, horns, or claws. If you get them extremely upset or frightened, however, they may spit at you, but that happens very rarely. Alpacas are social, communal animals that stick pretty close to home, requiring minimal fencing. They even have the courtesy to leave their droppings in communal piles, making cleanup a breeze.

Alpacas are pleasant to be around and can be profitable to raise, but they do require an initial investment. Even buying one male and two female alpacas to start a herd can be quite costly, considering that the average price for a female ranges from between $12,000 and $25,000, and a top-quality male can go for between $20,000 and $50,000. Lower-priced animals are available, but they typically don't generate the profits of their higher-priced counterparts.

AT A GLANCE

Salary Range

The average salary range for farmers and farm managers is between $32,000 and $59,000, according to government figures. Depending on the size and type of operation, however, alpaca farmers have the potential to earn much more.

Education/Experience

No specific experience is required, but because farming requires business skills in addition to knowledge of animals, it's a good idea to have a bachelor's degree in business with a concentration in agriculture or farm management.

Personal Attributes

Some people consider alpaca farming to be a lark, but it's serious work. You'll need to be willing to work hard and provide constant care for the animals, even if it means staying up all night with a female about to deliver her cria (a baby alpaca). You'll also need to be organized in order to effectively run and market your business.

Requirements

Anyone can buy a few alpacas and declare himself an alpaca farmer, but some practical farm experience probably will be required if you're raising alpacas for someone else. Many people who get into farming have grown up in farm families, or have participated in youth agricultural programs, such as 4-H youth educational programs. If you decide to set up an alpaca farm, remember to check out your municipality's zoning requirements. Zoning officials frown on farms established in areas not zoned for agricultural use.

Outlook

While farming jobs in general are expected to decline between now and 2012, a bright outlook is predicted for some types of niche farming such as raising alpacas. Most income for alpaca farmers currently is generated by breeding services, but the industry is working hard to expand the market for alpaca fleece, which would provide even better financial opportunities for farmers.

If you want the real *crème de la crème* in alpacas, however, you'll need to be prepared to spend much more than that. Particularly desirable females have brought prices of $50,000 or more. And the most desirable males have been sold for more than $150,000. In fact, at an auction in 2002, a particularly unique male was sold for $265,000, setting a world record.

Once you've made the initial investment, however, the cost of raising alpacas is fairly low. It costs only about $25 a month to care for an alpaca, about half the cost of raising a cow. That's partly because alpacas love to graze on leaves and grass, which means they don't require as much feed or hay as some other animals. And alpaca farmers can benefit from lowered property taxes on land that's classified as farmland, and may be eligible for income tax refunds for animal depreciation.

Breeding the animals and selling the offspring generates the primary income associated with raising alpacas, but some alpaca farmers keep the offspring until they begin to produce offspring of their own, thereby compounding the alpaca herd. Then animals may be sold selectively from among the herd.

As of 2003, there were only about 42,000 alpacas in the United States, nearly all of which are registered with the Kalispell, Montana–based Alpaca Registry, a system set up to assure that alpaca breeds remain pure, and are not cross-bred with

Jack Grebe, alpaca farmer

Jack Grebe more or less fell into a job that is turning into a career better than anything he could have hoped for. At just 19 years old, Grebe manages the Flying Pony Alpaca farm in Boyertown, eastern Pennsylvania. The farm currently has 44 alpacas, and Grebe is having the time of his life caring for the animals and seeing to the additional work of running a farm.

"I can't imagine anything better," Grebe says as he looked out over the alpacas grazing in the pasture. "It's beautiful out here, especially when the sun shines. This has turned out to be the ideal job."

Grebe graduated from high school in 2003 and had done some landscaping work on the alpaca farm. He expressed his interest in working with animals and, having already proven himself to be a good worker, was offered the job of managing the farm. The rest, as they say, is history.

Grebe, who knows each alpaca by name, has great affection for his herd. He says each animal has a different personality, and he enjoys watching them interact and play with one another. "It's fun to watch them together," he says. "They assign themselves a herd order. I think that she's number one at the moment," he says, gesturing toward a large female named Diadem. "She sort of leads everyone else."

Young alpacas, Grebe says, play a version of "King of the Hill" on dirt mounds in the pasture. He's gotten to know their sounds and signals to one another, such as an alarm call that sounds much like the honking of a goose.

Although Grebe had no formal training when he took the job, he's quickly learned the ins and outs of alpaca farming. He reads everything he can get his hands on, talks frequently with other alpaca farmers, and attends seminars and shows.

their llama cousins. The selective breeding and long gestation periods (11 months) of alpacas helps to control their numbers and keeps the demand for the animals high.

There also may be some income potential from selling the alpaca's fiber, which sells for up to $5 an ounce. However, the fiber market has not reached its potential, primarily because there are no commercial alpaca wool processing plants in the United States. Nearly all the fiber is sold to small, cottage businesses.

If you're interested in starting your own alpaca farm, you may have to look for investment capital or find loans to get started. Alternatively, you can begin by managing someone else's alpaca farm. For example, there are a fair number of people who have started alpaca farms on their land for tax purposes, and they aren't all that interested in the work entailed in running a farm. The Alpaca Owners and Breeders Association provides a directory of alpaca farmers throughout the United States.

It's also possible to buy shares in an animal and let it remain at its home farm. This lets you get into the alpaca business even if you live in the city, without a farm in sight!

Pitfalls

Alpaca farming, like any other kind of farm work, is demanding and can be stressful, especially if an animal gets injured or becomes ill. The hours are long,

Grebe spends his time feeding the animals in the morning and again at night, keeping them watered, cleaning and tending to the pastures, maintaining fences, keeping up the barn, and doing paperwork. He also shows the alpacas, hoping to win ribbons that will increase their value. He looks forward to the early spring shearing of the animals, and knows which of the alpacas' fleeces is likely to generate the most income. He also enjoys seeing the crias—baby alpacas—being birthed, and helping to care for the young animals.

Cold weather chores include laying stall mats for the animals so they won't have to lie on cold stone, and making sure the barn stays open at night so the alpacas can come inside when they want to. You also need to feed them more hay in the winter because there's less food for them to graze on outdoors.

"There's always stuff to be done," Grebe said. "But sometimes I get a chance on a rainy day to sit down and read. And that's good, because there's always more to learn."

Flying Pony Alpacas is a member of the Alpaca Owners and Breeders Association, and Grebe enjoys interacting with other breeders and farmers to keep up with the latest trends and industry advancements. His first love, though, remains the animals. And it seems that the alpacas are becoming increasingly comfortable having Grebe in their midst.

"They're shy animals, and when I first started here I would walk into the barn and they'd all run out of the barn into the pasture," he said. "But now I can walk into the barn and they just stand there waiting for me."

and the job requires a lot of physical labor. Income may be limited until a herd has increased in size and there are animals to sell or breed.

Perks
Alpacas are gentle, delightful animals that are fun to be around. Most alpaca farmers find joy in being with their herds. And once you get established in the business, there's good opportunity for financial success.

Get a Jump on the Job
If you can find an alpaca farm near you, chances are the farmer would be happy to let you get hands-on training by helping to care for the animals and do general farm work. If you're lucky, he or she might even be willing to pay for your help. You also can learn a lot about alpacas by reading, and there are numerous regional organizations that are affiliated with the Alpaca Owners and Breeders Association. A list of the organizations is included on the association's Web site.

BEEKEEPER

OVERVIEW

For some, it's the perfect horror story: the luckless fellow garbed in veil, gloves, and coveralls, covered by a tossing, moving wave of bees. But to the apiarist, it's just another day on the job. Apiarists—that is, beekeepers—operate beehives to produce honey and other products, and to have the bees pollinate crops. As you can imagine, beekeeping is not without risks and challenges, but many find it to be exciting and rewarding work.

The scope of a beekeeping operation can range from just a few hives in the backyard to hundreds of hives as part of a commercial operation. Most beekeepers start with a relatively small number of hives, adding more as they gain experience and start earning money.

Each hive contains a colony of bees plus the queen. When the colony gets too big, about half the bees will fly away and look for a new place to live. This is called swarming, and occurs in the early spring and summer. While some beekeepers buy colonies of bees, others prefer to retrieve swarms that have left their colony, using them to colonize a different hive. Retrieving these swarms, which normally gather on a tree limb while scout bees are out looking for another nesting site, can be a tricky proposition, but it's a good way to enlarge your business.

The daily chores of a beekeeper depend on the season, weather, and what's going on in the hives. During the winter months, there is very little outdoor work required, but a beekeeper can use that time to build and maintain equipment, attend beekeeper

AT A GLANCE

Salary Range

Beekeeper salaries range from a few thousand dollars to 10 times that much, depending on whether the beekeeping operation is full time or part time, its size, location, and other factors. Of the estimated 190,000 beekeepers in the United States, only about 4 percent depend solely on bees for their incomes.

Education/Experience

No formal training is required, but it's a good idea to take beekeeping classes and join an association of beekeepers. A Master Beekeeper program was developed at Cornell University and expanded by the Eastern Apicultural Society of North America. Those awarded the Master Beekeeper Certificate are competent at a college level in the three areas where they are tested. Any experienced beekeeper is eligible to apply for certification as a master beekeeper, if they have a minimum of five years of experience as a serious beekeeper in some aspect of apiary management. Applicants also should have completed the equivalent of a college-level course in beekeeping, and have a letter of nomination by a current master beekeeper, professional beekeeping specialist, or current president of a local, state, or regional beekeeping organization.

Personal Attributes

You'll need to be a hard worker to be a successful beekeeper, and able to withstand a lot of physical activity. In addition, you should not be allergic to bee stings if you wish to keep bees, because stings do happen with some regularity. You must be willing to work irregular (sometimes long) hours, and you should be comfortable spending long periods of time by yourself. You should enjoy being outdoors, and not uncomfortable working in isolated areas, where bees sometimes swarm. In short, beekeepers are generally a hearty bunch who are not afraid to get their hands dirty.

(continues)

AT A GLANCE (continued)

Requirements

Various state laws govern many aspects of beekeeping. For example, many states prohibit bringing in bees on comb or even used bee equipment without an entry permit. Other states require licenses to keep bees, enabling the state to make inspections of the honey operations. Check with your state on specific laws governing beekeeping.

Outlook

While agricultural jobs in general are projected to decrease by about 15 percent by 2012, the U.S. Department of Labor's Bureau of Labor Statistics does not offer an outlook specific to beekeepers. The outlook on beekeeping may depend on where you live, how many beekeepers are in the area, and other factors.

organization meetings, and read up on the latest industry news and innovations. If you need to purchase bees, you should order them in January or February.

By March, the queen bee is steadily increasing the rate at which she lays eggs, and it's necessary to check to make sure the bees have an adequate food supply. If a hive's honey stores are low, you'll need to do some emergency feeding to prevent the bees from starving to death. As spring blossoms appear and the bees begin to move about and bring pollen into the hive, a beekeeper's daily tasks increase. Hives need to be regularly inspected, cleaned, and maintained. Each colony of bees should be tested to see if mites are present, which must be treated if they are. You need to monitor egg laying, swarming, nectar flow, and honey robbing by wasps or other bees.

August and September are honey harvest months, when honey is taken from the hives and processed to be sold. Careful records must be kept on the amount of honey harvested, packing, shipping, and so forth.

Fall chores, in addition to honey harvesting, include making sure the bees have enough food for the winter, medicating the hives and preparing them for the winter by covering them to keep them dry, installing a wind break, and so on. Beekeepers also perform tasks such as building and repairing hives, transporting hives, removing honeycombs from the hives and extracting honey, and packaging honey and other bee products.

There's also a business side to beekeeping. You'll need to be able to negotiate land use with farmers or other landowners if you're unable to keep your hives on your own property. Regulations concerning beehives vary, depending on where you live, so be sure to check with municipal officials before you go out and invest in beehives. Often, a farmer will be happy to let you keep beehives on his property, because the bees pollinate crops. In fact, some farmers are willing to pay to have bees on their properties. It's also important to keep good records concerning the bees, hives, and honey. (You need to track the ages of the bees, for instance, so you'll know when it's time to replace the queen bee.)

People have been keeping bees for centuries, but that's not to say the business is without modern innovations. You can buy computer software to help track every aspect of your beekeeping operation and to record detailed reports of the hive's output (both hobby and professional versions of the software are available).

Pitfalls

Unless you can find used equipment, the cost of getting started in beekeeping can be steep. And because new bee colonies don't produce much excess honey in the first year, it can take several years before you see any profit from your hives. Moreover, you've really got to like this job, because beekeeping involves work throughout the year—even when the bees aren't producing

Dana Stahlman, retired beekeeper

Dana Stahlman of Blacklick, Ohio, has spent his entire life around bees. Growing up in a commercial beekeeping family, he learned early on about patterns of the queen's eggs, honey supers, and swarming.

Recently retired, Stahlman is still used to long days and hard work among his beehives. During his busiest time working in Ohio and Georgia, he operated 600 colonies of bees. And he still works as a consultant for a beekeeping operation with 1,700 colonies. Even though he's retired, Stahlman is well known and active in the beekeeping industry, and is still in the business of raising and selling queen bees. He also offers an online beekeeping course, and a beekeeping course on a compact disc.

"It takes a lot of work to keep bees alive and healthy," Stahlman says. "Beekeepers spend a lot of money on various treatments to keep bees alive, and it's not getting easier. The mites that attack honeybees have built up a resistance to the chemical in the products used by the beekeeper, making them harder to control. There's a lot involved in caring for bees."

While Stahlman found beekeeping to be extremely enjoyable and rewarding, he warned that it's not easy—nor a career for someone who's looking to get rich quick. "Commercial beekeeping is a farming operation, and one getting into it must have working capital as well as an inventory of bee hives and equipment," Stahlman says. "It's not for anyone wanting to make a fast buck."

Someone interested in becoming a beekeeper should seek out a job with a commercial beekeeper and learn about the business from the ground up, Stahlman advises. You can buy books on beekeeping, and some colleges and universities offer beekeeping technician programs. If you're starting out on your own, start small, he says, and expand as you're able to. Consider all the business aspects of the operation, such as additional equipment that you'll need as you expand and extra help you may need to hire.

While beekeepers can be trained, Stahlman said, successful ones are born with a deep affinity and appreciation for bees. "My mother told me that my grandfather had me in the bee yard by the time I was one year old, and it just became a part of my life," he says. "It was what I was supposed to do, not something I ever had to think about."

Stahlman said he can tell early on which of his grandchildren are potential beekeepers. "The most important event with young ones is their first bee sting," he says. "I watch how they react to it, and if they're willing to return to the hives on their own afterward. If they do return, I know I have a potential beekeeper. If they don't, I still love them just the same. But I'd never force any of them to be around the bees. They all understand that bees sting, and they either put themselves in harm's way or they stay well away from the bees."

any honey. You could end up working hard for a long period of time without realizing any profit.

Perks

Keeping bees provides built-in adventure and challenge, which makes it appealing to some people. If you enjoy being outdoors and working on your own, and have a special interest in honeybees, you could be very happy as a beekeeper. Honeybees are fascinating creatures that are extremely interesting to study.

Get a Jump on the Job

Join an apiary group or organization so you can meet other beekeepers, and ask to tag along to help tend to the hives, gather swarms, check on the bees, and perform other tasks. This will give you an overview of what's involved with beekeeping. It's also a good idea to learn some carpentry skills if you're going to be a beekeeper. This cuts expenses by allowing you to build and repair your own hives.

In addition, check out courses offered by beekeeping organizations and some university cooperative extension offices, community colleges, and junior colleges. Some beekeepers simply learn about the trade from others in the field or by reading instructional materials, but generally, some formal training is desirable.

BUFFALO HERDER

OVERVIEW

They're some of America's last remaining cowboys, going up against a herd of animals weighing between 1,000 and 2,000 pounds on a daily basis. And since buffalo don't like to be told what to do, herding them comes down to your will against theirs.

Ancestors of the American buffalo (which are really bison, not buffalo at all) have roamed the earth for hundreds of thousands of years. They used to travel across the entire North American continent in herds of between 500 and more than half a million animals. It's hard to imagine that in just a short time, excessive hunting and exploitation of this mighty animal nearly led to its extinction, but by 1889 there were fewer than 1,000 buffalo left in North America. After a concerted effort to save this historic breed, today the numbers hover around 350,000 and are growing.

Since buffalo have had more than their share of unfortunate contact with humans, it's not surprising that they've never gotten used to being around people. That's why when a buffalo herder tries to make them do something or go someplace they may not want to go, it can get very tricky. One Kansas buffalo herder summed up the situation nicely: "You can drive a buffalo anywhere he wants to go."

Buffalo herders are a busy lot, and the work never ends. When the grass is growing in the spring, the buffalo must be moved around frequently so they don't deplete the grass in any given area. There's also a lot of fencing work during the spring months. In summer the herders work to get the corrals ready for the fall roundup, when buffalo are herded into corrals to be given ear tags, worm medicine, and vaccines. Maintaining grasslands and making sure the land remains productive are daily tasks.

While buffalo herds used to be managed entirely on horseback, more and more herders today are turning to motorcycles. While buffalo don't particularly like motorcycles, they're not nearly as opposed to them as they are to horses. Horses and buffalo have never gotten along, and using horses to herd them is dangerous because of the risk of buffalo charges. Herding buffalo with horses is not only hard on the buffalo herder (or *buffalero*, as some of

these rare-breed ranch hands prefer to be called), but on the horse as well. Buffalo herders can go through four or five horses a day because the work is so demanding for the animals.

Although most of us tend to see buffalo as slow, lumpy, lumbering animals, in fact they're as agile as deer and can outrun horses. They're not the kind of animals you want to mess around with.

Most of the buffalo in the United States live on private ranches, and the rest are legally protected in Yellowstone Park or in refuges such as the National Bison Refuge in Montana. Because of the increasing

Ken Klemm, buffalo herder

Ken Klemm grew up around wild animals, working as a trapper, packer, and wilderness guide. He understands animals and has a great respect for all of them, but none more than the American bison. "They're the king of the prairie," he says fondly.

In the past, he's worked as foreman on a 120,000 acre ranch with 3,500 buffalo, herding buffalo with horses (and later motorcycles), spending long hours completing ranch work. A typical day started at 7 a.m. and lasted until it was too dark to see what you were doing, working five days a week and half a day Saturday. While the work was hard and the hours long, Klemm thoroughly enjoyed his days as a buffalero. "The neat thing on the ranch was that there was no average day," he says. "Every day was different and you never knew what was going to happen."

These days, Klemm keeps about 150 buffalo on his 462-acre ranch north of Goodland, Kansas, raising them to be sold and slaughtered. He and partner Peter Thieriot own a company called The Buffalo Guys, which markets buffalo meat and meat products such as buffalo jerky, buffalo hot dogs, and buffaloaf. Klemm's tasks tend more toward managing the buffalo meat business, but he still enjoys the times when he can saddle up his horse and roam his ranch, checking out the grasslands and the buffalo that occupy them.

The thing to remember about buffalo, Klemm said, is that they're wild animals. "We've been domesticating cattle for six or seven thousand years," he says. "We've only been keeping buffalo for the past 40 or 50 years, and they're not used to being around people. Buffalo don't tame down the way cattle do."

For that reason, he says, herding buffalo is dangerous work. "Buffalo don't like it when you try to mess with them," he said. "They try to kill you."

In addition to herding, the work of keeping a buffalo herd involves maintaining grasslands and making sure the land remains productive. "Basically, we're in the grass business out here," Klemm said. "It's all about watching the land. We're always learning more about it."

popularity of buffalo meat as a healthy alternative to beef, there's an increasing demand for people willing to work with the animals. In fact, most ranchers raise buffalo to sell as a source of food, making it necessary for herders to round them up and corral them so they can be sent out for slaughter. In addition, some ranches open their lands to private hunts at certain times of the year.

If you work as a buffalero, you could commute to and from the ranch you work for, but many herders live on the ranch in quarters set up for workers. You might get lucky and get a private cabin, but often ranch workers live in communal bunkhouses. It can be tough in other ways: Because the work of tending a ranch never stops, you can't expect to work a nine-to-five day and just head for home. Work normally begins early in the morning and doesn't stop until nightfall. Buffalo herders usually are expected to help with other ranch work as well, including installing and mending fences, monitoring grassland, making sure the animals have enough water, tending to irrigation, maintaining buildings, and so forth.

Herding buffalo isn't for everyone—but if you're a hardy type who loves

The buffalo on Klemm's ranch are left to themselves as much as possible to assure that they don't become dependent on man. Other than getting ear tags and the yearly de-worming and vaccinations, they're pretty much left alone. The animals breed and birth on their own schedules and calves nurse for as long as they wish, without being weaned from their mother's milk. No growth hormones or therapeutic medicines are administered to the animals, which live almost as naturally as the original American buffalo herds.

"I suppose some day buffalo could become domesticated, but I'd hate to see that happen," Klemm said. "They're wild animals. That's what makes them so healthy. I guess it all depends on how they're managed."

The buffalo aren't the only ones that benefit from being left alone, Klemm said. It's also better for the buffalo herders.

The animals breed in the fall, which means there's always some mean bulls around. The cows calve in the spring, and the mothers get fiercely protective of their offspring. Buffalo herders know very well how important it is to watch their backs.

"There are no fat, slow buffaleros," Klemm says. "You've always got to be ready." Whether herding buffalo on horseback or with motorcycles, you've got to be prepared for a charging animal. "Buffalo hate horses," Klemm says. "They absolutely hate them. So they charge them all day long. They're not wild about the motorcycles, either, but they don't chase you all the time when you're on one. That's why we all learned to use the motorcycles."

Herding buffalo is tough work, but probably doesn't require any specific courses, Klemm says. If you're going to run a ranch in addition to herding animals, however, he suggests that you consider getting a business degree. Otherwise, the best plan is to work on two or three large ranches to learn the business of herding buffalo and maintaining the property. "Learn everything that you can about wild animals and nature," Klemm says. "That can't ever hurt."

adventure, and the idea of being out on an open prairie sounds appealing, it might just be your cup of tea.

Pitfalls

Buffalo herding can be dangerous: Buffalo are wild animals—unpredictable and defensive when facing a perceived threat. The job also is extremely physically demanding, and you might have to give up some privacy if you're required to live in communal housing on the ranch where you're employed. Days off might be hard to come by.

Perks

Working on a ranch gives you tremendous freedom. Imagine traveling over hundreds of acres on horseback or motorcycle, enjoying the open prairie and endless sky. Most ranch workers have a good deal of respect for the animals they tend, and enjoy working with them. And because good ranch workers are in demand, you probably can expect fairly good benefits as part of your compensation package.

Get a Jump on the Job

The best way to learn about buffalo herding is to work on a ranch where buffalo are raised. If you're not at a point in life where you can do that, you can get a head start by learning all you can about wild animals. Spend time outdoors where you can watch animals in their natural habitats. There also are good books and informational Web sites about buffalo that can get you started.

BUG WRANGLER

OVERVIEW

Think it's hard to coax a trick out of a cockroach? Try getting a fly to wash its face on cue. It's all in a day's work for a bug wrangler—a specialist whose job it is to ride herd on the tiny insect actors in films, TV shows, or commercials.

Most bug wranglers start out as entomologists (scientists who specialize in bugs), and have branched off into the movie/TV/commercial business because of their expertise.

Typically, they are experts in insect behavior, so they can consult with producers and directors about getting bugs to act in certain ways for the camera.

While it's not generally possible to train a bug, if you know how a bug would normally react, it's possible to arrange a situation to make it look as if it's been trained. In addition, bug wranglers are often called upon to provide particular insects for a project: If a director needs a certain type of butterfly, it's a lot easier to call up a bug wrangler than to grab a net and go out into the wild and try to find the insect.

Your typical day as a bug wrangler would start when a director or producer would call, asking if you could manage to get your hands on a bucket of ants, a hive of bees, or a clutch of cockroaches. Or maybe the production company already has the insects, but needs you to figure out how to get a bug to jump up and down, wash its face, or crawl over a piece of paper.

If you take on the job, you'd pick up a copy of the script or take a look at

AT A GLANCE

Salary Range
Extremely volatile, but can top $100,000 year.

Education/Experience
Degree in entomology or biology, specializing in insect behavior.

Personal Attributes
Attention to detail, patience, ability to work with insects and humans, excellent oral communication.

Requirements
None.

Outlook
Limited. Movie industry heavily tied with economy, and computer animation may limit future jobs in this field.

the storyboard, and consult with the director about whether the project is even possible—and how to change it if it's not. Once you're all agreed on what you'll be doing, you work with the insects (if needed) or collect any required bugs, and then you show up on set for the actual bug work.

Pitfalls

The economic situation in the movie industry and the increasing amount of computer animation in films today may mean there would be fewer opportunities to wrangle bugs in the future. The job also can mean lots of hard work in unpleasant weather conditions.

Perks

What could be more fun than working on movie sets with famous actors and playing with bugs—and getting paid really well

Steven Kutcher, bug wrangler

Steven Kutcher gets paid to play with bugs—and he's made a successful career as the bug expert for a whole slew of popular movies. It's Kutcher who watched over the carpenter ants covering actress Sigourney Weaver in *Copycat*, a swarm of African locusts in *Exorcist II: The Heretic*, giant mosquitoes in *Jurassic Park*, a tarantula in a costume in *James and the Giant Peach*, and stampeding spiders in *Arachnophobia*.

It's all in a day's work for Kutcher, who favors a trademark red *Bugs Are My Business* baseball cap. He's taken care of 3,000 African grasshoppers for six months and kept 6,000 large darkling beetles in his living room. He's had to make a cockroach run across the floor and then flip over on its back, make a spider climb into a slipper from four feet away, have a butterfly fly free in front of a logo, make bees swarm indoors, release 1,000 butterflies at a wedding, and make a live wasp fly into an actor's mouth. Think that was easy? In May 1995, he went to Australia to work on a movie called *Race the Sun*—where he had to teach a cockroach to pop up out of a shoe on cue, walk up to a bag of Cheetos, and then wander onto a surfing magazine and stop on a picture of a surfboard.

But movies make up only a part of his wrangling business. He's also managed insects for a variety of music videos, including Paula Abdul (a display case of butterflies), moths in Christina Aguilera's *Fighter*, mealworms and scorpions for Alice Cooper, and a cockroach for Billy Idol's *L.A. Woman*. His commercial jobs have included managing butterflies for AT&T, bees for Gladlock, a praying mantis for Polaroid, a snail for Apple Computer, and many more.

Kutcher has been featured in more than 100 national magazine articles, and appeared on TV and radio programs including *The Tonight Show* and *The Late Show with David Letterman*. In 1990, *National Geographic* produced a short documentary on his work in education and the film industry.

Of course, there's no "bug wrangling" major in college, so Kutcher started his career in a much more typical fashion. He'd been interested in natural science as a kid spending his summers in the Catskills, living close to nature, picking berries, canning food. "I liked those things, and so at an early age I knew I wanted a career that had something to do with nature," he remembers. He went on to earn a B.S. in entomology from the University of California–Davis, and a master's degree in biology specializing in entomology, insect behavior, and ecology at California State University in Long Beach. In 1974 he began teaching entomology and insect ecology at Long Beach State College, and since then he's taught biology for non-majors at five different community colleges. In 1978 he taught a class in cultural entomology, focusing on the relationship between insects and man. In the past, he's done summer work for two mosquito abatement districts, fly studies for the Los Angeles sanitation district, and consulted on stored grain products for private industry. He's also initiated an entomology lecture series and started the annual Insect Fair at the Los Angeles State and County Arboretum.

By getting his entomology degrees, he was able to amass a lot of tools he could use in his later career. "I was planning on getting my Ph.D. and being a research entomologist," he recalls. "I had to work very hard, because I didn't start out as a good student. But I became an exemplary student, and I also learned about photography, art, communicating, and teaching."

And then, in 1977 a professor recommended him for insect work in *Exorcist II*—and he's never looked back. For that film, Kutcher had to provide 3,000 African locusts. "I jumped in with a major feature film and I thought that was the end of it," he recalls. "I did a few commercials and movies." And then one day he started counting how many films featured insects. "I discovered that one out of every three movies had insects in them. Nobody had noticed that before. Everybody looks at the same thing, but it's what's inside your head that makes it different. I saw what everybody else saw, but I also saw something *more*—I saw an opportunity. If I could provide even a fraction of the insects for the entertainment world, that's a lot of potential."

Kutcher then noticed that film companies hired animal trainers to handle not just the chickens, cows, and horses, but also snails, ants, and spiders. "In reality, what they really needed was someone to handle snails, ants, and spiders separately. If you go to the hospital, you wouldn't say: 'Just give me a doctor who does everything.' You'd want a specialist. Same with the movies. I saw a need, and I saw that I could fill that need," he explains.

When he starts work on a film, he first consults with the director. "I tell the director: 'You're not going to get ants to walk in a line, but you can simulate a line of ants.' If I don't consult with a director, they are going to get on the set and find out that they can't get a line of ants to do what they want."

Because of his entomology training, he knows a lot about insect behavior. When he needed to make a fly clean itself on cue, he first experimented with sprinkling a little talcum powder on the fly. "But the dusty fly did nothing—he just sat there. Then I tried powdered sugar, and the fly still just sat there. But I knew that flies taste with their feet, so I got some honey and dipped the fly's feet and head in the honey. As soon as I sat the fly down, he rubbed his head where the honey was."

The other part of his job is to actually provide insects. "If you need an insect, I know how to raise it, get it, or catch it," he says.

Kutcher has wrangled insects for at least 75 feature films, along with countless commercials and TV shows. The last big movie he did was *Spider-Man*. "With the current economy and the changing film industry, the amount of work for a bug wrangler has diminished. Many of the jobs are going to Canada, and computers are providing more of the insect images. Economically, things are very tight in Hollywood."

As Hollywood work gets tighter, he's begun to focus more on the environment, teaching at the Audubon Camp in Wyoming, and handling ecology weekend workshops for the Sierra Club and many other programs and training sessions. He created a traveling entomology program for primary and secondary schools that has included presentations of more than 400 programs ranging from experimental entomology to insect habitats. Today, Kutcher says he's working for a better environment. And aware of the relentless onslaught of computer animation, Kutcher is looking to enlarge his business.

"Successful people generally have three characteristics," he says. "They are passionate about their work, the timing has to be right, and they have to be doing something different. In high school, you spend a lot of time trying to be like everyone else. In the real world, being different is important. People who really make a difference walk the road less traveled."

"What I like best about my work is that I get to solve problems and go on all kinds of adventures," he says. "My real passion is studying and trying to improve the environment. To study the Earth, one must be close to it and cherish the value of life—and that includes insects."

for it? If you love insects and you enjoy working for yourself, this job is ideal.

Get a Jump on the Job

If you've got a yen for bugs and think you might like to work with insects in the movies, you can start out by learning as much about bugs as possible. Visit your local library or bookstore for volumes on insects and various types of bugs. Then think about applying for an insect-related summer internship. Searching the Internet for "insect summer internship" will reveal tons of neat possibilities. For example, check out:

* San Francisco Zoo's summer Insect Zoo internship: http://64.233.161.104/ search?q=cache:S7O_wDkB3XQJ: www.sfzoo.org/jobs/+insects, +internship&hl=en&ie=UTF-8
* North Carolina State University's Summer Internship Program's Insect Biological Control Projects: http:// www.cefs.ncsu.edu/intern/intern_ projects/insect.htm

CHRISTMAS TREE GROWER

OVERVIEW

A career as a Christmas tree farmer is one of those romantic jobs that attract people with visions of Currier and Ives–like holiday scenes drifting through their minds. But it's not all happy families choosing the perfect tree and money clanging into the cash register. Growing Christmas trees is a year-round job that requires fortitude and lots of hard work. You also need to be aware that it takes between six and 12 years to produce one marketable Christmas tree, which is why many experts recommend that you have a secondary, income-producing crop when first starting out in order to generate money before your first tree harvest.

If all that doesn't dampen your enthusiasm, you'll need to start growing your Christmas trees from seeds planted in beds or greenhouses. Most tree farms, however, don't grow their own seedlings; instead, they buy them from producers when the trees are about two years old and ready to be planted in the field.

Once the trees are planted, you can't sit back and wait for the trees to grow and the money to roll in. Christmas trees require a significant amount of care and attention to keep them looking their best. Small trees are at risk of being crowded out by weeds and other plants that steal their space and moisture, and it's important to keep competing plants under control. It's also necessary to prevent disease and control insects that can seriously damage small trees, and

AT A GLANCE

Salary Range

The average earnings of a full-time Christmas tree farm manager working for an employer were $43,740 in 2002, with a range of between $32,620 and more than $81,100. Many Christmas tree growers, however, rely on income from their tree businesses as secondary income and have other jobs to provide their primary income.

Education/Experience

Any sort of hands-on experience in an area relating to agriculture or forestry is useful and applicable. While many growers learn from other growers and depend on supplemental information from their local cooperative extension service, there are college programs that are very helpful if you're considering growing Christmas trees as a business. Some growers earn business degrees with concentrations in agriculture, while others obtain agricultural degrees.

Personal Attributes

Curiosity and willingness to learn about forest management ranging from tree physiology to marketing are necessary for one to be a successful Christmas tree grower. You'll also need to be determined, willing to work very hard, and be constantly attentive to environmental factors.

Requirements

None.

Outlook

Unfortunately, the market for real Christmas trees is growing smaller as artificial trees become more popular. In 1990, half the Christmas trees found in American homes were the genuine article, but by 2003, only 30 percent of all Christmas trees were real. As the population continues to age, sales of real trees are expected to continue to decline. However, some growers feel that the trend toward artificial trees will reverse as growers continue to make advances in the appearance and cleanliness of the trees.

to be on the lookout for rodents that strip the bark from the young trees.

In addition, all trees must be pruned annually in order to protect them from disease and to shape them in that familiar conical Christmas tree shape. As with just about all types of farming, growing Christmas trees is not without risk. Drought, insects, and other pest infestations and problems can seriously jeopardize a tree crop and slash the grower's profits. A particularly bad series of problems can put you in the red for the whole year. Constant attentiveness is required to minimize the possibility of catastrophe.

Ever mindful of the slow march toward artificiality, Christmas tree growers continue to make improvements in the ease of using real trees that are more and more appealing to customers. Many growers have invested in equipment that drills a hole into the bottom of a tree so that it

William Swingle, Christmas tree grower

William Swingle grew up on a Christmas tree farm, counting the days until he could go off and do something else. Yet when he left his parents' farm after college to go to another part of the state to work as a construction manager, he was surprised at how much he missed the land and the sky and the trees.

Now, at age 34, he's back at Spring Brook Century Farms in Mansfield, Pennsylvania—the place where he grew up. He lives with his own family in a house that's belonged to his ancestors since the 1800s, growing and selling Christmas trees with his brother, Robert, on the farm they purchased from their father.

While Swingle thoroughly enjoys life as a Christmas tree grower (he also teaches shop in a high school near his home), he admits that it's very hard work and there's not that much money to be made. "I'd say it's probably the minority of growers who do it full time," he says. "For most of us, it's just not lucrative enough to do as our only job."

During busy seasons in the Christmas tree business, Swingle estimates that he works 40 hours a week at his teaching job and at least another 30 at the tree business. The long hours, he said, are just the nature of the business—and it's not just the December holidays that require his attention.

After December, the work starts up again in spring—tree-planting time. With 225 acres and about 40,000 trees at any given moment, Swingle estimates they plant between 3,000 and 5,000 seedlings every April. Then throughout May, it's time to carefully inspect their trees for problems. "Basically, you get fungus, insects, and weeds that can hurt the trees," Swingert says. "Those are the things we stay on the lookout for."

The summer months are very busy, because mowing and shearing the trees are full-time jobs, and every able hand is recruited to help. During September and October, Swingle and his brother trim the tops of the trees, and tag the trees that are for sale. In mid-November, they start cutting the nearly 2,000 trees that will be shipped out for sale in other parts of the state, often working into the night to get it done. The trees get shipped off a couple of days after Thanksgiving, after which the rush is on for customers to come to the farm to buy trees, along with the swags and wreaths that Swingle's wife makes.

Customers, some of whom have been getting their trees at the farm since Swingle was a boy, can cut their own trees or buy them precut. If they're looking for atmosphere, customers

can simply be placed on a spindle mounted in a large pan, eliminating the need for tightening a tree stand to avoid a wobbly tree. Most growers also have invested in machines that shake dead needles out of the trees and that automatically wrap trees for easy transport. Still other farms include petting zoos, hot chocolate stands, and Christmas tree ornament stores on their property. Some invite local charities or groups (such as Scouts) to offer food stands, selling hot dogs and sodas to hungry tree purchasers. Visiting Santa Clauses, hayrides, tractor rides, and other entertainment are also added inducements to attract families to consider the purchase of a Christmas tree as a holiday experience.

Pitfalls

Farming of any kind can be unpredictable and frustrating, often because of

can hitch a ride out into the fields on a hayride, or use their own car to drive down the lane into the fields. The objective, Swingle says, is to make the experience as pleasant and hassle-free as possible.

Once the Christmas rush is over, Swingle spends January and February culling out bad trees, doing paperwork, and planning the buying and planting schedules for the rest of the year. While he doesn't feel overburdened with paperwork, it's necessary to keep good records of seedlings purchased, the number of trees that survive, how many trees are cut and shipped, how many are sold on site, how much income is generated, and so forth. "It sure helps to be organized and have a little bit of business sense," he says.

Swingle and his brother realize how lucky they were to have a ready-made farm available for them to buy, because he wonders how someone looking to get into the tree growing business would be able to do so without making a very large investment.

"The thing is, the areas that are good to grow trees also tend to be prime development areas," he explains. "That makes the land very expensive to buy."

And the length of time between the time you plant your trees until you can make any money from them can be daunting. "If you're starting from scratch, you have to wait 8 to 10 years to get any money back," Swingle says.

If you're interested in owning a Christmas tree farm and your parents don't already own one, Swingle suggests that you might want to get a job on an established farm that belongs to someone who may be looking to retire in the not-too-distant future, and negotiate to buy or take over the farm after the owner retires. Or, you could plant some trees on your own property and farm part time, depending on a salary from another job as your primary income.

Swingle worries about the increasing popularity of artificial trees, but hopes that the trend may reverse itself. Natural trees still are in demand, and he's betting on the fact that many people are realizing an artificial tree just isn't a satisfactory substitute for a real one. "We'll see what happens," Swingle says. "I'm not really worried. Not too many people around where I am have artificial trees. They might be easier, but I think a lot of people still know there's nothing better than a real tree."

circumstances beyond your control. If you're self-employed and you own a Christmas tree farm, you'll need to have your own insurance and retirement savings plans, which can be difficult to fund when you're first starting out.

Perks

If you relish the thought of transforming a small seedling into a beautiful Christmas tree that will bring joy to someone's holidays, chances are you're considering a career that you'll find satisfying and rewarding. Growing Christmas trees is great for someone who loves being outdoors. What's more, your customers are generally upbeat and happy when they come to buy their Christmas trees, which makes selling a pleasurable task.

Get a Jump on the Job

Check with your area cooperative extension agency about courses or programs about Christmas tree growing that might be helpful. If you know a grower, you could find out if you might serve as an apprentice, or send letters to area growers expressing your interest in the career and asking if there are any positions available. In many states there are associations that support Christmas tree growers, in addition to the National Christmas Tree Association (check Appendix A for contact information).

CITRUS GROWER

OVERVIEW

When you're a citrus producer, one thing's for certain: You never know what you'll be up against, one day to the next. Temperatures might take a sudden dive, forcing you to take emergency measures to save your crop. You might have a season of record rainfall—or a drought. Citrus fruit is subject to various diseases and pests, making disease and pest control a daily issue. As if all that isn't enough, you could get a hurricane season like the one in 2004, where some citrus growers in the so-called Sunshine State experienced four hurricanes in two months.

That's not to say that citrus production isn't a rewarding—and potentially profitable—business. Citrus growers, as other farmers, experience tremendous satisfaction from a successful crop, working as farmers have worked for thousands of years to nurture produce to harvest. In the United States, most citrus production is concentrated in Florida, California, Texas, and Arizona, so if you don't enjoy a warm climate, it might be a good idea to re-examine your career goals.

While many people think citrus growing is a seasonal endeavor, there's work to be done all year long. When you're not harvesting fruit, you must tend to the groves and equipment, replace ailing trees, and keep up with the day-to-day demands of running a citrus business. As in many industries, citrus production is becoming increasingly dependent on technology,

AT A GLANCE

Salary Range

The median salary for citrus growers in 2002 was $376 a week, but there was a wide range between the lowest 10 percent at less than $226 a week to the highest 10 percent at more than $822 a week. Salary will vary depending on the type of work and success of a particular crop.

Education/Experience

Anyone can plant some orange, grapefruit, or lemon trees and call him- or herself a citrus grower, but to successfully run a citrus-producing business, a degree in agriculture (preferably combined with a business-related degree) is highly recommended. You probably wouldn't be able to get loans for start-up money without at least a bachelor's degree in agriculture or business, or a combination of the two.

Personal Attributes

You need to be able to think on your feet, making quick decisions when necessary to assure the health of your citrus crop. Physical endurance is important, because you'll be working long hours at different times of the year. You should be organized and business minded, and not afraid of hard work.

Requirements

Citrus growers are subject to strict disease prevention and food safety standards. Growers must be licensed and meet requirements set by the U.S. Department of Agriculture, and possibly state and local regulatory agencies.

Outlook

Employment is expected to decline by about 15 percent between now and 2012, according to the U.S. Bureau of Labor Statistics. Even some citrus producers are not optimistic about the future of the industry, as reported in the July 5, 2004 edition of the *Naples* (FL) *Daily News*. Citrus growers cite declining demand for orange juice and imported citrus products as reasons behind the bleak forecast.

so ongoing education and training is an important issue.

Harvesting occurs between late October and the end of May. Although there are some automated picking techniques, many growers hire pickers to harvest the fruit by hand, using ladders and picking bags. Once picked, the fruit is dumped from the bags into field bins, which allows it to be easily loaded onto harvesting trucks. Harvesting trucks carry the fruit to the packing house, where it is washed and rinsed, and then examined for defects such as decay or scarring. A natural wax is applied to preserve the fruit. Automatic sizing machines separate the fruit according to circumference and send it to separate packing bins, where

Matt McLean, citrus grower

Matt McLean was born into a Florida citrus-growing family. His great-grandfather raised citrus and cattle. His grandfather sold the cattle to go with citrus fruit full time, and his father followed suit. McLean grew up in the citrus business, so staying within the industry seemed like the natural thing to do.

Understanding the complexities of the citrus industry, McLean earned a degree in business administration from the University of Florida in Gainesville. His first venture after graduating was to return to his hometown of Clermont and start a juice brokerage business, which means he matched up citrus growers with orange juice producers.

His career path was to change, however, when a German customer asked McLean about importing organic orange juice. McLean was intrigued by the idea of organic juice, especially since his great-grandfather and grandfather had advocated growing citrus without the use of synthetic pesticides and fertilizers. After researching the topic, McLean decided to become a citrus grower.

He now grows citrus on 400 acres in various areas of Florida. The idea, he said, is to avoid having all your crop in the same location in case a problem occurs. "You never want to put all your eggs into one basket," McLean said.

Most of McLean's crop is used to make juice sold under an "Uncle Matt's Organic" label.

McLean advises anyone interested in citrus growing to consider a college education. Growing citrus is a business, he explains, and business skills are necessary in addition to agricultural knowledge. "I'd say that college probably isn't mandatory, but it certainly is preferable," he says. College options include a business administration degree, as McLean has, an agricultural/economics degree, or even something as specialized as a degree in fruit crops.

McLean acknowledges the difficulties of citrus growing. There is significant pressure from disease, pests, cold and freezes, and, he points out, Florida soil is not particularly good. "The soil isn't rich down here because we're on a peninsula," he explains.

Still, McLean is happy to be following in the footsteps of his ancestors. "We're excited to be farming some of our own groves and doing what we do best," McLean said. "That's building healthy soils and healthy trees that will in turn yield the best quality fruit. We're ensuring the superior quality of our fruit—hands on."

workers pack the fruit according to size. Once packed, the cartons are placed into cold storage until it's either sold as citrus or sent off to be made into juice.

Summer months in the citrus-growing industry entail work such as summer fertilizing, pruning dead wood from the trees, mowing weeds, and pulling vines from the branches of the citrus trees.

If your heart is set on being a citrus grower, you'll need to prepare carefully for the career and be knowledgeable in all aspects of the job. Even though growing citrus fruit entails challenges and frustrations, it still can be a good career, allowing you independence and resulting in a sense of accomplishment and pride.

Pitfalls

Growing citrus fruit can be at the very least unpredictable, which makes for unpredictable income from season to season. Even in a successful growing season, the work is hard, with long hours. Citrus is ripened on the tree, and when it's ripe, you've only got a narrow window to get it picked and transported to its next stop.

Perks

If you enjoy working outside and thrive on challenges and hard work, you might just love being a citrus producer. Agricultural work allows you to operate independently, make your own decisions, and call the shots regarding your crop. Some innovative citrus growers have been quite successful financially.

Get a Jump on the Job

If you live in a state where citrus is grown, you can join your local citrus growers' association, at least as an associate member. If you live in citrus-growing territory, you also may be able to get a job on a citrus farm and begin learning the business from the ground up. In citrus states, 4-H or agricultural programs in your school offer courses or projects dealing with growing citrus.

CRAB FISHERMAN

OVERVIEW

Crabbing may sound like some sort of Hemingway adventure—heading out to the open sea in the predawn mists, with the salty spray in your face and the wind in your hair, returning a few days later to pull up those pots and collect your treasure. But the reality is far less romantic: For the crab fishermen who risk their lives to put a pile of steaming crabs in front of hungry diners, their job involves 18- to 20-hour days working in bone-chilling waters and unpredictable weather.

The basic job of crabbing is pretty much the same whether you're fishing off the West Coast for Dungeness crab, or on the tamer East Coast for the Chesapeake Bay blue crab—also known as jimmies, callinectes sapidus, channelers, sooks, and she-crabs.

If you hire on as a crabber, here's what you'll do: You'll motor mile after mile, pulling up steel-framed crab pots that have been dropped days earlier, each baited with pieces of squid. Many crab fishermen use a hydraulic winch to haul up the pots off the side of the boat. Sometimes you'll get lucky and find several crabs in one pot; sometimes the pots are empty. In any case, once the pots are emptied, you rebait the pots, drop them back in and move on.

Average catch for an average crab boat is about 1,500 pounds of crab. Fishing for crabs hundreds of miles from shore with commercial vessels requires a crew that includes a captain or skipper, a first mate

AT A GLANCE

Salary Range

Between $300 and $700 a week.

Education/Experience

In most cases, no formal academic requirements exist. If you can pilot a boat and haul crab pots, you're qualified. Upper level positions on large commercial vessels require training specific to each job.

Personal Attributes

Good health and physical strength; good coordination and mechanical aptitude; perseverance to work long hours at sea, often under difficult conditions; the ability to assume any deckhand's functions, on short notice. Must be able to work as a team member, and must be patient, always alert, to overcome the boredom of long watches when not engaged in fishing operations. The captain must be experienced, mature, and decisive and also must possess the business skills needed to run business operations.

Requirements

Captains of large vessels over 200 tons must be licensed by the U.S. Coast Guard; captains and mates on large crab fishing vessels of at least 200 gross tons must be licensed. Captains of sportfishing boats used for charter, regardless of the boats' size, also must be licensed.

Outlook

Job opportunities for crab fishermen and crab boat operators are expected to decline in coming years due to the depletion of fish stocks and new federal and state laws restricting both commercial and recreational fishing. Even with quotas, crabs are being caught at a faster rate than they can reproduce, and fewer crabs translates into fewer crab fishermen. With crab stocks declining and catch restrictions increasing, job openings will occur primarily as the result of retiring workers.

and sometimes a second mate, a boat-swain (called a deckboss on some smaller boats), and deckhands with specialized skills. Small, self-employed fishermen are the captain, mate, deckhand, and lumper (laborer) all in one. On a large commercial boat, you'll probably just have one of those jobs.

The captain oversees the operation, and makes sure the vessel is seaworthy; he or she also oversees the purchase of supplies, gear, and equipment, obtains all the required permits and licenses, and hires and manages the crew. The captain also plots the vessel's course using electronic navigational equipment along with the more traditional compasses, sextants, and charts. The captain directs the operation and records daily activities in the ship's log. Back home, the captain arranges for the sale of the catch and doles out the pay.

The first mate is a sort of captain's assistant (or copilot), who can take control of the vessel when the captain is off duty. The mate's regular duty is to direct the operations and sailing responsibilities of the deckhands, including the operation, maintenance, and repair of the vessel and the gathering, preservation, stowing, and unloading of the catch.

The boatswain is an experienced deck-hand who supervises other deckhands as they sail the vessel. When necessary, boat-swains repair gear and equipment, and make sure decks are clear and clean and that the vessel's engines are working well. Unless lumpers (laborers or longshore workers) are hired, the deckhands unload the catch.

More than half of all crabbing workers are self-employed. Most people learn the trade from their fathers or grandfathers, but you don't need to be born to a crabbing family to get into the business. Crab fishermen can learn the job after a few months of training, working next to an experienced worker.

Some full-time and many part-time crab fishermen work on small boats in relatively shallow waters, often in sight of land. Crews on these boats are small; one or two people usually handle all aspects of the operation.

Although most crab fishermen are involved in commercial fishing, some captains and deckhands offer their boats for charter, for periods ranging from several hours to a number of days.

Crab fishermen work under some of the most hazardous conditions of any occupation, made more serious because help is often not readily available when emergencies occur. Malfunctioning equipment can lead to collisions or shipwrecks; malfunctioning gear can cause injuries, as can slippery decks, ice formation in the winter, or being swept overboard. If that isn't enough, crab fishing vessel operators face strenuous outdoor work and long hours.

Earnings of crab fishermen vary widely, depending upon their position, their ownership percentage of the vessel, the size of their ship, and the amount and value of the catch. The costs of the fishing operation (including the fuel costs, repair and maintenance of gear and equipment, and the crew's supplies) are deducted from the sale of the catch and net proceeds are distributed among the crew members in accordance with a prearranged percentage. Typically, the ship's owner (usually the captain) gets half, but from this amount the

Zach Rotwein, crab fisherman

Ever since he was a kid, Zach Rotwein was fascinated by fins and claws—and couldn't imagine a better life than living on the sea, catching fish and crabs for a living. Today he's captain of the Sundown, a 30-foot fishing boat, and the proprietor of Cap'n Zach's Crab House in McKinleyville, California. And since modern technology has reached the crab world, he even sells his catch online.

Some years he makes a very good living—other years he's lucky to break even. As for most people who make their living on the sea, crabbers need a good price and lots of crabs to make a good living. In a good year, Rotwein can harvest thousands of pounds of crab in a few hours. An off year might require him to toil for 12 hours or more on the water for less than 600 pounds. "The secret used to be to go out and fill your boat," he says. "Today the secret is to go out and get as many crab as you can—and then get the most money for them." It's a competitive lifestyle that can be grueling. "You gotta get out there, fish long hours, fish in rough weather," he says. He remembers when he's stayed up 42 hours straight crabbing, crashed at home for four hours of sleep, and went back out again. "There are only so many crabs out there," he says, "and while you're sleeping, someone else is pulling them up."

Rotwein fishes for Dungeness crab, and at the moment the fishery operates on a different system from most others—there are no limits on how many crabs you can catch. You can't harvest female crabs and males under six inches. This way, male crabs can reach sexual maturity and mate, and females can carry those eggs to term. So what the California crabbers are after are legally sized male crabs—and he who tries hardest gets the most before the supply is exhausted. When the season opens in December, boats steam back to port carrying tons of crab each day; by the end of the season in early summer, you're lucky to find 300 pounds a trip. The job is made more difficult because you've also got to pay for gear, bait, fuel, and labor—not to mention those fixed costs, like boat and engine maintenance, boat insurance, docking and license fees, and boat depreciation. One crab pot alone can cost $100. A crab fishing license can run $16,000.

Crabbing got so competitive that Rotwein figured he might want to figure out a way to bring in extra cash. "I heard all these people complaining about the quality of the seafood around here," Rotwein says. He knew there were plenty of crabs, because he was bringing them in each day—he just needed a way to get those crabs to market. "I saw a niche," he says. That niche—his crab house—has helped cushion him from the ebb and flow of the crab industry. "Running the crab house isn't as exciting as catching the stuff, but in a bad year I have another job," he says. Rotwein crabs because he says it's "the most relaxing thing I can do." But to succeed as a crabber, you also have to be a tough, tenacious businessman. "What we have left are high-bred crabbers, the ones who are capable of surviving a couple bad years. The ones that will survive are the ones who are doing something right."

owner pays for depreciation, maintenance and repair, and replacement and insurance costs of the ship and its equipment. What's left is the owner's profit.

Operators of large commercial fishing vessels are required to complete a Coast Guard–approved training course. The U.S. Coast Guard issues these documents and licenses to individuals who meet the stipulated health, physical, and academic requirements.

Pitfalls

If you ever wondered why crab is so expensive, one important reason is that the men and women who risk their lives fishing for crab in the freezing waters off Alaska and the western coast of the United States face one of the highest on-the-job mortality rates. It's dangerous because each boat carries 5,000 to 10,000 pounds of crab pots, which can make the boat unstable, especially when the pots are being set out in the water. In addition, crab fishing is strenuous work, takes long hours, and provides only seasonal employment. Although newer vessels have better living quarters, with TV and on-board showers, crews still must cope with the aggravations of confined quarters, continuous close personal contact, and the absence of family.

Perks

Call it the allure of the open sea, but most people who make their living on the open ocean love the independence and freedom—and also the danger. Most crab fishermen will tell you they've known people who have died doing this work. But they continue to go after the crab precisely because of the challenge and the danger. It's a kind of adventure only crab fisherman know.

Get a Jump on the Job

The best way to find out what it's like to be a crabber is to hire a sport crab fishing boat and see what it's like. Seasonal jobs as helpers are also sometimes available. You can also enroll in two-year high school vocational-technical programs in crab fishing technology, and some community colleges and universities offer fishery technology and related programs that include courses in seamanship, vessel operations, marine safety, navigation, vessel repair and maintenance, health emergencies, and crab fishing gear technology. Courses include hands-on experience. These secondary and postsecondary programs are normally offered in or near coastal areas.

CRANBERRY FARMER

OVERVIEW

What would Thanksgiving be without a big bowl of glistening jellied cranberry sauce? While most Americans down the stuff during the winter holidays, we don't give much thought to where these little red fruits actually come from, or how they get from bog to bowl.

The cranberry—*Vaccinium macrocarpon*—is a native American fruit, a member of the heath family and cousin to the blueberry and huckleberry. The Pequot Indians of Cape Cod called the berry *ibimi* ("bitter berry") and made pemmican by mixing cranberries with dried venison and fat. They also used the little red fruits as a fabric dye and medicine. When the Pilgrims arrived, they dubbed the red fruit a "craneberry" because they thought the small, pink blossoms that appear in the spring resemble the head and bill of a Sandhill crane. European settlers adopted the Native American uses for the fruit and used the berry as a valuable bartering tool, although the Pilgrims didn't start cultivating them until 1816, when a bog was planted and tended in Dennis on Cape Cod. By then, American and Canadian sailors had learned that eating cranberries would protect them from scurvy, much the way that eating limes protected the British "limey" sailors.

Today, cranberries are commercially grown throughout the northern part of the United States and Canada, and are available in both fresh and processed forms. Contrary to popular belief, however,

cranberries don't grow in water. Instead, they pop up on trailing vines in impermeable beds layered with sand, peat, gravel, and clay typically found in New England wetlands. These beds, commonly known as *bogs*, were originally made by glacial deposits. Cranberries are a finicky sort of fruit, only able to survive under a very special combination of factors: an acid peat soil, an adequate fresh water supply, sand, and a growing season that stretches from April to November. The bogs are dry most of the year as the berries grow on short vines. Most cranberries are harvested between September and October, either by wet or dry harvesting.

By far the most common is wet harvesting, where the bogs are flooded and motorized pickers knock the hollow berries off the vines and they float to the water's surface for easy harvesting. The floating fruit is then corralled and loaded onto trucks. Wet-harvested fruit is used for processed cranberry products such as juice and sauce.

If the farmer chooses to dry harvest, the bogs don't get flooded. Instead, the fruit is combed from the vines using a mechanized picking machine, and then loaded into bins and shipped to receiving stations where it is cleaned and packaged as fresh fruit.

The cranberry season begins in winter when growers flood the bogs with water that freezes and insulates the vines from frost. As the winter snow melts and spring arrives, the bogs are drained. Shortly thereafter blossoms begin to appear. In mid-July, petals fall from the flowers leaving the tiny green nodes that, after weeks of summer sun, become red, ripe cranberries. Cranberries are typically harvested in September and October and can be stored for up to one year under proper conditions.

Planting begins in April, when farmers replant sluggish beds by mowing plants in other beds, laying the mowed cuttings on the new bed by tractor spreader. Cranberry vines sprout from these cuttings. A mechanical planter follows the spreader, pushing the cuttings into the ground, where they will grow for four to five years before being ready to harvest. Normally, however, growers don't have to replant because an undamaged cranberry vine will survive indefinitely. In fact, some

Cape Cod vines are more than 150 years old. Sometimes a bog may be replanted because the bog may not be level, the variety doesn't produce well, or weeds (such as briar or poison ivy) have overtaken the vines. In such cases large construction equipment is needed to move the soil, leveling the bog in preparation for planting new vines.

In the spring, the vines are green and red-green buds (called *uprights*) grow on the woody stems. During the spring and summer, farmers mow the areas around the banks of the bogs, cutting down anything that will shade the plants, which would slow down plant growth. In June, the appearance of pink and white cranberry blossoms prompt farmers to hire beekeepers to bring in their bees to spread pollen. As the blossoms die, green pinheads appear that will eventually become the berries.

For the rest of the summer, the farmer is on the lookout for pests, until October, when the red berries are ready to pick. If the farmer opts for wet harvesting, the beds are flooded one at a time, followed by reels driven through the beds to churn up the water and knock off the berries, which float to the surface. A floating boom corrals the berries, where they are then placed on a conveyor belt to be funneled into barrels.

U.S. cranberry production is big business, averaging half a billion pounds each year—and growing. Although the little red berries are harvested from the Atlantic to the Pacific, top producers are located in Wisconsin (53 percent of all cranberries), Massachusetts (30 percent), New Jersey (8 percent), Oregon (6 percent), and Washington (3 percent). Other top production states include Michigan,

John Andresen, cranberry farmer

Cranberry farmer John Andresen got his first good look at Massachusetts cranberry bogs from 1,000 feet up in the air, as he flew toward the ocean as part of his job as a swordfish spotter for private fishermen. "I used to do lot of flying," he recalls, "and I'd see the bogs from the air. They just looked so beautiful! It looked like a cool way of life."

The next thing he knew, some of his friends actually bought some bogs, back when cranberry prices were at an all-time high, fetching $50 to $60 dollars a barrel. "I was getting tired spending my life in the middle of the ocean all day, so I bought some bogs, too," he says. John and his wife Doanne founded Duxbury Cranberry Farm, what is now one of the area's larger growers, offering fresh cranberries for sale on order, and also as a pick-your-own bog in late fall. His own bogs are at least 100 years old—not unusual in this part of Massachusetts, where well-cared-for cranberry plants can last almost indefinitely.

Andresen grows three varieties of cranberries out of the hundreds of different kinds available, divided into two basic types: earlies and lates, depending on whether they ripen in early September or mid-October. Most of his berries are sold to Ocean Spray, and the rest go to Decas Cranberries, a small local company.

Although cranberries have been growing in Massachusetts bogs for centuries, those grown commercially do require some tending. Andresen applies about an inch of sand on the bogs every three or four years, fertilizes every summer, and protects them from the cold. When the temperature plummets below 10 degrees and the north wind kicks up, cranberry growers flood their bogs with water to keep the plants from drying out. "When the cold air comes down from Canada, the cranberries are susceptible to winterkill," he says. "All the moisture will get sucked out of the leaves and they'll die. So we flood the bogs, submerge the plants in water, and the ice protects them." Once ice forms on the bogs, Andresen hops on a sand buggy, drives out on the ice, and lays down sand on the ice. When the ice eventually melts, all the sand drops down on the bog.

If the plants are submerged for more than a month, however, the oxygen level drops too low, so constant measurements help warn the growers to drop the water level and let the plants breathe from time to time.

Minnesota, Rhode Island, Maine, and Delaware.

Pitfalls

As with many other types of agriculture in the United States, cranberry farmers are buffeted by controversial attempts at market controls, dropping prices, and rising costs. Smaller, hobby farms went out of business in the price war of 1997, and prices per barrel are still slow. It costs $30 to $35 a barrel to grow cranberries, and in 1997 the price a farmer earned dropped to a low of $10 a barrel. Today, the price has risen to about $40 a barrel. Added to the economic considerations are growing competition from Canada and Wisconsin, in addition to new varieties of plants capable of doubling per-acre yields, which risks flooding the market with the tiny red fruits.

"My advice to new farmers is don't pay too much for bogs, because the market in New England is very unstable. I'm really uncertain what's going to happen to us in the future, with the threat of [increasing production of] berries [from growers outside New England]."

Andresen survived the plunge in cranberry prices in the late 1990s by doubling his acreage. "Instead of having 26 acres, we leased another 31 from people who were retiring." Because of the low prices, the farmer couldn't sell his berries, so he simply rented his land to Andresen. "The bottom line—it's the same story with every farming business in this country. The prices go down, and the only way people stay in the industry is by taking on more acreage. It's the same thing out in the Midwest. Every time that happens, a lot of farm families have to stop farming. I never thought it would happen in the cranberry industry."

In response, cranberry production companies are frantically trying to open up new markets in Europe. "People see that there is some money to be made growing cranberries," Andresen says. "And Canada subsidizes farmers, helps make them new bogs, so they can grow cranberries for less there. It's a big threat to us in the United States."

Despite the hard work and the frustrating and uncertain outlook for the future of cranberry growing in the United States, Andresen still loves his job. "The lifestyle is just great," he says. "It gives me an incredible amount of freedom. I don't have to punch a clock—when I want to go fishing, I go fishing. When I want to go skiing, I can go skiing. That's the best part of it."

Of course, there is hard work at times. "But it's seasonal," Andresen explains, "so there are periods where I have to work very hard, and other periods where I don't have to work at all. I live on 70 acres of land, I have a beautiful house, and it's just really pretty. I would never have been able to build this house without the cranberry bogs." Andresen also loves watching the wildlife as well. "We have birds, coyotes, foxes, red-tailed hawks, deer, geese, bluebirds—every kind of bird you can think of. The Audubon people would go nuts here."

"It's an old style way of living that's typical in this country, but that's getting to be more and more threatened. But it's a fun, unique way of life and I wouldn't trade it for anything."

Perks

Living the life of a cranberry grower is ideal for someone who loves the outdoors and working in nature. Cranberry bogs are wetlands, and therefore attract a wide variety of birds, waterfowl, and wildlife. Because the work is seasonal, there are times when the grower has plenty of free time to enjoy the rural lifestyle.

Get a Jump on the Job

If you live in a cranberry-producing area, see if you can help out during busy seasonal times. Experimental stations and cooperative extensions linked to state universities in cranberry-producing states often feature helpful seminars, workshops, and information sessions on the latest in cranberry production.

CROP DUSTER

OVERVIEW

Crop dusting (more commonly known today as aerial application) began in the early 1920s when an Ohio pilot flying a surplus World War I Curtiss JN-6H plane—known as a "Jenny"—dumped a load of powdered lead arsenate onto an orchard plagued by the Catalpa sphinx moth, a pesky critter that was wreaking havoc with Ohio's fruit crop. The process wiped out the moths, elevated the pilot to hero status, and kicked off the modern practice of crop dusting.

The mechanics of crop dusting have changed a lot in the past 80 years, as have the planes used to deliver the chemicals. Crop dusting disperses pesticides, fungicides, or fertilizers onto crops, and it's also used to apply pesticides in areas containing standing water or other conditions favorable to mosquitoes in efforts to control West Nile virus. Crop dusters also may be used to seed areas in which erosion is a problem.

If you want to be a crop duster, you must have an excellent understanding of not just airplanes, but weather and wind patterns. Too little wind tends to cause the chemicals to float about, making it difficult to predict where they'll land. Too much wind causes too much drift.

Some crop dusters work for established companies, while others own their own planes and manage their own business. If you choose the latter route, you'll have to

AT A GLANCE

Salary Range

The median annual earnings for crop dusters ranges from less than $26,100 to more than $200,000.

Education/Experience

Crop dusters are commercial pilots, so you'll need to have a commercial pilot license; to earn a commercial pilot certificate, you first need to earn a private pilot certificate or its equivalent, and an instrument rating. Most aerial application planes are tailwheel planes and require different flying skills from the more common nosewheel planes, so you'll need to be trained in tailwheel flying.

Personal Attributes

Pilots sometimes encounter stressful situations with changing weather or conditions, and must be alert and able to act quickly when necessary and be able to handle stress.

Requirements

To earn a commercial pilot's license you must pass stringent medical exams; be at least 18 years old; be able to speak, read, write, and understand English; have a commercial pilot's license; have 20/20 vision (with or without glasses); have good hearing; pass written exams on safe flight and navigation techniques; and prove your flying aptitude to Federal Aviation Administration (FAA) examiners. You'll also need to learn the specifics of crop dusting.

Outlook

The airline industry was plunged into turmoil after the 9-11 attacks on the World Trade Center and the Pentagon, and it has not yet fully recovered. As a result, many airline pilots have been laid off and may be competing for crop dusting jobs. Still, pilot jobs in all categories are expected to increase at about an average rate through 2012, and, with the proper training, you'll have a good chance of landing a job.

Ted Stallings, president of crop-dusting company

Ted Stallings learned how to fly a plane when he was 11 years old and has been flying ever since. Following in his father's footsteps, he became a crop duster, eventually taking over his father's business, Aero-Tech, Inc. Now 46 years old, Stallings will tell you that times have changed in the crop dusting business—starting with the name.

"We don't call it crop dusting so much anymore," Stallings said. "We're known today as aerial applicators. When you say crop duster, you tend to think of a guy with a scarf around his neck flying in a little plane and dumping out dust to wherever it happens to land. It's not like that anymore."

There have been many other changes in the profession, in addition to what it's called. While Stalling's father bought his first plane for about $17,000 and declared himself a crop duster, the planes the company purchases today cost about $1.2 million—each. The planes—the company's aircraft of choice is the Air Tractor turbine AT 802—are loaded with the latest technology and far bigger than the little plane Stalling's father first used. As a result, more training is required to fly them, resulting in a real demand for crop dusters.

"It used to be you could get yourself a plane and just take it out," Stallings said. "If you came back, then you were a crop duster. But today, there's so much technology involved with the planes and with the business, pilots need to be trained. There's a need for pilots and there's going to be more and more of a need. These pilots are in big demand."

Fertilizing and forest protection and maintenance are the mainstays of Aero-Tech's business. Company pilots have been sent to fight forest fires in Chile, Algeria, Guatemala, Alaska, and elsewhere, earning the company a widespread reputation for excellence. While aerial application work is exciting, always different, and can be extremely profitable, it's also quite dangerous, Stallings said.

"We lost our nephew last year, and I lost my best friend three years ago," he said. "It's like race car driving. Everybody in the business knows somebody who's died while they're doing it."

Because it's dangerous work, there's potential for error in spraying, and the cost of the aircraft is so high, getting and staying insured can be difficult, and the cost prohibitive, Stallings said.

Still, he said, it's a great business to be in if you love flying and want to make good money. It's not uncommon for pilots at Aero Tech to earn between $20,000 and $30,000 a month, he said. One pilot recently earned $48,000 in one month. However, Stallings warned, the work is seasonal, so it's important to be smart about spending and saving your salary.

While licenses and training is important, Stallings said, it's also important to get to know about the business of aerial application. If you can, hang around a company that provides crop dusting, and ask a lot of questions.

"Just get in there," Stallings advised. "Wash the airplanes or sweep the floor, just to get your foot in the door. You can go to crop dusting school, and learn to fly a taildragger. That's really important. But the most important things are that you love flying and you're willing to learn as much about the job as you can."

make a considerable investment before you can begin, because a top-notch crop duster can cost more than a million dollars. There are, however, smaller, older, less expensive planes available. If you're looking to start your own aerial application business, you'll also need to have good organizational and business skills and know how to go about marketing your business and working with customers. Knowledge of different pesticides, herbicides, fire-fighting substances, and other chemicals is also important.

Crop dusting today is much different and more sophisticated than it was in the 1920s, with today's planes built for higher spraying speeds and shorter take-offs. The modern planes, such as the Ayres Turbo-Thrush and the Air Tractor Turbo Crop Duster, also carry far more chemicals than their older, less maneuverable counterparts, allowing pilots to cover more ground in less time. Modern aerial applicator planes also are equipped with Global Positioning System equipment and computers that allow pilots to view flight plans.

To become a crop duster, you'll need to earn your private and commercial pilot licenses through a flight school that's certified by the FAA. Links to approved flight schools can be found on the Internet at http://www.globemaster. de/links/Flight_Training/Schools.

Pitfalls

If you have your own business, you not only have the initial cost of equipment, but ongoing insurance expenses, which tend to be very high. Increasing lawsuits over aerial applications of pesticides that landed in residential areas in waterways—killing fish—are driving up insurance rates and causing headaches for crop dusters.

Perks

If you love flying, working as a crop duster is a great way to log hours in preparation for a higher-paid regional or national airline pilot job. Even if you never go that route, spending your time doing something you love isn't a bad way to make a living.

Get a Jump on the Job

If you happen to know a crop duster, ask if there's room for you to ride along on a job. As him or her to explain the process of crop dusting. Learn about different chemicals crop dusters use and learn all you can about planes and aviation. If you've already turned 18 and have funds available, you can start working toward obtaining a private pilot's license—the first step toward reaching your career goal.

DEER FARMER

OVERVIEW

Most of us think of deer as wild animals roaming the woods and fields of rural America, offering us domesticated folk a haunting glimpse of wildness right in our backyards. But to more and more farmers, deer are offering a new livelihood as a type of livestock being raised on small farms and large ranches much like cattle. While wild deer still roam much of the United States, more and more niche farmers are realizing there's a good living to be had in managing these deer much like domesticated cattle, providing meat for venison lovers without the required days spent hunting for deer themselves.

And because deer don't eat as much as cattle, are less damaging to pasture grass, and take up less space, deer farming can be up to three times as profitable as traditional livestock. Deer also mature earlier than cattle and can continue reproducing for up to 20 years.

Farmed deer is North America's newest livestock, with the potential to boost a sagging agricultural economy. According to the North American Deer Farmers Association, farmers are raising deer in 46 states, accounting for about 65,000 deer of various species. Still, deer farming in the United States is concentrated in four states, where more than half of the farm-raised deer are found: Texas, New York, Michigan, and Wisconsin.

Deer farming in the United States got its start in the late 1970's, becoming more popular each year with aggressive

marketing. As consumers continue to worry about their waistlines, the demand for farm-raised venison continues to grow. Venison is a popular dining choice because it's low in fat with fewer calories than beef.

If you're interested in farming deer for a living, your first decision will be to choose the type of deer you're going to raise (you may need to consider your local laws and regulations). Non-native species of deer are excellent livestock with the capacity to efficiently convert pasture into healthy, lean meat. Fallow, red, sika, and axis deer are most commonly farmed in the United States, popular because of their strong herding instincts, efficient grazing, disease resistance, and adaptation to domesticity.

Once you find out what types of deer you can legally raise in your area, you'll need to consider the purpose for which you will farm them—as breeding stock, for meat or other products, or for hunts. Each species of deer is slightly different and are raised for different reasons.

Fallow deer are outgoing creatures that birth easily and are typically farmed for venison; they don't cross breed with other species of deer. Sika are similar to fallow deer in size and disposition and are also farmed for venison; they will cross with elk and red deer. The more temperamentally stable red deer are larger than fallow or whitetail deer, and will cross breed with elk or sika deer; they are also farmed for venison and for their velvet. Axis deer produce fawns year round, do best in warm climates, and are farmed for venison and for hunts. White-tail deer—the native North American wild species—do not cross breed with other farmed deer, and often produce multiple fawns. They are farmed for trophy and hunting stock. Elk deer, the largest of the farmed deer, will cross breed with red and sika deer, and are raised for velvet, as trophy stock, and for venison.

Once you've selected the type of deer you're interested in raising, you'll need to build or buy the right kind of handling facilities so you can handle the deer with a minimum of stress. These handling facilities include a series of pens, chutes, and squeezes that help control the deer for iden-

tification and health procedures. Typically, deer require certain vaccinations (depending on your state requirements); bucks must have their horns removed each year so they don't gore each other. Other than these basic chores, however, deer don't need much handling—usually only once or twice a year. For this reason, deer farmers can handle many animals without needing extra help. What's more, you don't need to worry about manure removal, elaborate barns, or exotic feed rations.

There are all sorts of things you can do with your deer herd in addition to raising the animals for venison. Some farmers use deer for breeding or trophy stock, or sell the hides and hard antlers. Others raise their deer to provide hunting opportunities. And some farmers sell the velvet from the antlers for medicinal purposes. Deer antler velvet is a mammalian tissue that renews itself every year, comprising the whole antler (not just the velvety skin). The remarkably swift growth of the stag's antlers is unique in nature. Deer and elk antlers are grown anew every year; they reach their full size, and then fall off so that this remarkable cycle of nature can repeat itself the following year. As the new antlers grow, they become thick and round and feel warm and spongy. When the antlers have reached their full size, the blood stops flowing through the tissues and the antlers begin to harden as the cartilage transforms into bone.

The velvet is harvested at its maximum nutritional and medicinal value while the antler is still in a cartilaginous state. The rapid growth of deer and elk antler from its velvet stage through to hard calcified bone has been the focus of intense scientific curiosity. Deer and elk velvet is also known as "velvet antler" and its alcohol extract is known as pantocrine. Whether or not the velvet is removed and sold, the farmer must remove the antlers for safety reasons, since stags normally become very aggressive during mating each autumn. If the antlers were not removed, they would pose a serious risk to both the deer and to the farmer.

The velvet is harvested under veterinary supervision using anesthetics, and is then frozen before being dried for export to Asia, where proponents believe the velvet has health properties ranging from increased stamina and promoting healing after surgery, to preventing osteoporosis and arthritis. Income from velvet is not available to European deer farmers, whose governments have banned the practice of velveting, reputedly on animal welfare grounds. The New Zealand, Australian, and North American industries have

Dan Brand, deer farm owner

Dan Brand grew up on a farm, working and raising cattle as his father did before him. Working with Angus beef on his 256-acre farm in Lewiston, Minnesota, he began thinking about diversifying as the agriculture business became more competitive. Several of his buddies in the area began raising deer for a living, and Brand thought about adding some deer to his operation. But by nature a cautious farmer, he spent the next five years reading everything he could find about deer farming before taking the plunge in 1994.

Today, his Brand Deer Farm sells and buys white tail breeder bucks, does, fawns, and bottle-fed fawns, and has been in the business since 1994. "We started out small," Brand recalls, "with only a few deer. But we're growing bigger every year." Brand Deer Farm now has 53 deer in addition to an Angus herd, and a sizeable hog operation.

A member of the Minnesota Deer Association, Brand concentrates on raising great quality white tail deer with excellent genetics. He works with breeding stock, and sells his deer to other deer farmers, in addition to renting other farms where he plants corn, peas, and beans. In Minnesota, a farmer can get a license to raise deer if they have a clean record with the state, with no deer hunting violations.

Brand feeds his deer a special mixture of food, and keeps them in two pens—one of ten acres and the other six acres. Minnesota requires that he vaccinate and test his herd every year for three years, for tuberculosis and for other diseases. "We're a closed herd," he explains. "We don't take anything from the wild." In fact, so tame are some of the deer that Brand's son can hand feed them, since they were bottle-fed as fawns. Each deer is named and easily identifiable. "I try not to get attached to them," said Brand's wife, "but they're just like your children."

The best part of the job, Brand says, is just watching these once-wild creatures grow up and live far longer lives in captivity than they would in the wild. In captivity, deer may live to be at least 15 years. "We have a doe here that's 13 years old," Brand says. "We call her Lena, and she's one of the first deer we ever got. We put the kids on her back and she'd give them rides.

"Wild deer never get a chance to grow up," he says. "It's interesting to watch them as they grow from two and three years. It's just so enjoyable to watch them."

responded to welfare concerns by putting in place mandatory velvet harvesting standards for farmers, underwritten by the veterinary profession.

Pitfalls

The primary pitfalls are hostile neighbors who sometimes shoot deer in the pens, release expensive breeding stock, or tear down fences.

Perks

You have to love animals and the outdoor life if you're going to be a farmer of any sort, since the responsibilities for taking care of live animals never stops. Many beef farmers now turning to deer say they're far more interesting and enjoyable to raise; simply watching the animals and working with them as they grow provides great satisfaction for many farmers.

Get a Jump on the Job

If you think you'd like to raise deer as a career, you can try to get a summer job helping out at a deer farm in your area. If you live in rural parts of the country, your local 4-H might help you raise your own deer as a project, which can help give you an idea of what's involved.

DOWSER

OVERVIEW

Some say it's magic. Some claim it's a gift, not a skill. Others insist it's a type of psychic power or voodoo.

No one knows for sure why—or even if—dowsing for water really works. Skeptics observe that there's so much water under the earth's surface that anyone with a forked stick could find it. But proponents point out that many times, well drillers have come up dry, only to hit water after a dowser has been called in for advice.

Dowsers were celebrated in African cave paintings some 6,000 to 8,000 years ago, but the first detailed description of mineral dowsing came in a 1556 description of German mining techniques in Germany. Using a branch to look for minerals was adapted to water dowsing during the reign of Elizabeth I in England. A U.S. Geological Survey pamphlet on dowsing notes that the practice has been almost unanimously condemned by geologists and technicians. Many cite experiments that show dowsers scoring little higher than random guesses in controlled conditions.

Those who believe in dowsing attribute the force to a wide range of causes, including electricity, empathy, magnetic fields, the chemistry of the body, or simple belief. The American Society of Dowsers says anyone can do it, but many dowsers disagree. What proponents do agree on is that dowsing makes it possible to consistently and accurately locate groundwater aquifers of all kinds, in all geological environments, before drilling, with a degree of precision far beyond the capability of even the best geophysical instruments.

Some say eight out of ten people who grab a stick in each hand can find water; others insist it's a rare gift available to only one in a thousand.

The tools of this controversial calling aren't fancy or high-tech, but typically, dowsers disagree on the best equipment for the job. Traditionally, a dowser reaches for a willow or maple branch with a slingshot crotch, or the sucker off an apple tree. Others use metal L-shaped rods of copper or steel, gripped tightly below the bend. Still others swear by two metal L-shaped rods made from two metal coat hangers (the longer piece of each L needs to be as long a straight wire as you can get out of the coat-hanger, and the other part of the L needs to be much shorter and at right-angles to the long length).

AT A GLANCE

Salary Range
$75 to $150 a session for independent consultants.

Education/Experience
No specific education required; experience in dowsing helpful.

Personal Attributes
Sensitivity, interest in working with people.

Requirements
None.

Outlook
As development continues and the need to locate water becomes ever more crucial, it is likely that the call for dowsers will continue as well.

Of course, you don't have to use a rod at all. Keys, scissors, and even a pair of pliers have all been used to dowse. Other dowsers use a pendulum—maybe a simple hex nut secured on a string—or a fresh shoot off a tree, a sturdy wire, even the plastic tip of a fishing rod.

But no matter what material you choose, the basic method is the same: You hold the two rods one in each hand, wrapping all your fingers around the short lengths without gripping them tightly. The long lengths are allowed to point forwards and kept roughly parallel to each other and the ground, as you walk slowly forward. When you pass over an underground water source such as a water or drain pipe, the rods will cross over one another. The feeling is unmistakable and irresistible.

If the dowser uses a traditional Y-shaped stick made of limber branches of willow, peach, or witch hazel, the sticks are held stem-to-sky, hands clutching the stick, palms up. The dowser squeezes tightly and starts walking until the stick bucks and twists on its own. Some dowsers' sticks point upward, toward the sky, while others head downward to the earth.

Some say they enter into an altered state of awareness when they dowse; some say they enter a trance; others focus on a mental picture. Successful dowsers say that there's no doubt about the pull of the water; it's impossible to stop the rod's movement, which can suddenly jerk and wrench as the dowser walks over underground water deposits. Large amounts of underground water can break a dowser's stick from the force.

Experienced water dowsers can accurately locate the best location to sink a new well; some also can determine the depth of the water, its drinkable quality,

Dean Stoltzfus, dowser

While dowsing may seem magical and mystical to some people, to Dean Stoltzfus the process is pretty much a down-to-earth process. Dean owns the water well contractors Petersheim Brothers in Morgantown, Pennsylvania, and he's been dowsing for water since 1984.

"When I bought the business, I just started dowsing," he explains. Stoltzfus uses two metal rods, walking in a pattern back and forth over the land. As he crosses over underground water—which usually happens within two or three minutes—the rods will suddenly begin to move. "I learned just by experimenting—just by doing it, and finding out what worked," he says.

He believes dowsing works by magnetic attraction, and he's been quite successful in locating underground water this way.

Whether you believe it works or not, the cost of drilling for water where no water exists makes it a good idea. "You don't have anything to lose by dowsing," Stoltzfus points out. "I don't have a problem if a customer wants to have it done or not have it done."

In Pennsylvania, where the company drills, Stoltzfus points out that drilling for water doesn't automatically mean you'll hit water—it's possible for a well to come up dry. "It doesn't usually happen," he notes, "but it's possible."

and the rate or volume of flow present at that spot. This is critical information, since drilling a new well can be expensive. For example, drilling a 400-foot hole without striking water may cost the homeowner about $10,000. Although dowsing isn't a guarantee, spending $75 to avoid losing thousands is a risk many homeowners and well drillers are willing to make. Many water dowsers have documented success rates well in excess of 95 percent.

Dowsers may work for real estate developers and private property owners, but by far their most typical client is a well-drilling company. Dowsing is also used commercially in the search for oil, minerals, and ore deposits. Many utility companies use dowsing to search for buried pipes and cables, and military uses of dowsing include the search for booby traps, mines, and unexploded bombs.

Pitfalls

Dowsing can be controversial, and not everyone will accept a dowser's skill. To be a dowser, it helps to have a thick skin to withstand the teasing of those who don't believe; you have to be willing to accept the fact that some people just won't believe you really can locate water.

Perks

The ability to find water by using such ancient means is a fulfilling and enjoyable occupation. You have the added benefit in knowing you are helping homeowners and possibly saving them lots of money in avoiding dry wells.

Get a Jump on the Job

Since there's no real school course you can take to be a dowser, you can learn more about the skill by watching an established dowser. Call your local well-drilling company or construction company and ask them for referrals to dowsers, and then find out if the dowser is willing to take on an apprentice.

EMU FARMER

OVERVIEW

Maybe you've seen them at a farm nearby, those silly-looking creatures with a long skinny neck popping out of a tuft of feathers. They're called emus, and since the 1980s, the emu-raising business has become popular across the United States. Emus are members of the ratite family—a group of large, flightless birds with a flat breast bone that also includes the ostrich, rhea, cassowary, and kiwi.

The emu is an Australian native, the second largest flightless bird in the world, standing between five to six feet tall, weighing 100 to 130 pounds. Able to live up to about 30 years, emus can swim, kick in defense, and run up to 30 miles per hour. Emus tend to be friendly and curious, following their owners around like puppies. The hair-like plumage of both sexes form a mop-like tail. At birth, chicks have longitudinal stripes, which eventually develop into a dark brown coloring of the neck and head, with beige and brown body feathers. Mature birds sometimes have a distinctive blue neck, with black feathers on the head and mottled body feathers.

Most experts agree the most productive way to breed and raise these birds is to pair up a male and female at about 18 months of age. Within the first one or two breeding seasons (from September through April) the pair will begin to mate and the female will start laying eggs, one at a time. The emu farmer then collects the eggs, placing them first into a special incubator for about 54 days and then into a hatcher.

AT A GLANCE

Salary Range

Income varies depending on location and size of farm, and whether or not the farmer also sells products. Those who sell emu products can earn more than $100,000 a year; those who only sell birds can earn a few hundred dollars for each bird. A number of companies dedicated to producing emu products earn more than a million dollars a year.

Education/Experience

Raising emus requires knowledge of these animals and their requirements. A degree in animal science is preferred and highly recommended.

Personal Attributes

Patience, love of animals, marketing, and business experience. Must be willing to put in long hours (sometimes in addition to another job) and have good business and organizational skills.

Requirements

None.

Outlook

Excellent. Many livestock experts believe that emu production has the potential to become an enduring new agricultural market that will continue to grow for many years ahead.

The female will continue to lay another single egg about every three days throughout the breeding season. You can expect each emu to lay up to 30 or more eggs per season.

There are several options for getting into the emu business. You could buy emu eggs and week-old chicks, or wait and buy chicks at 3 and 4 months old (either singly, or in pairs). Emu chicks aren't fussy about their living quarters and they're easy to raise—almost all chicks make it to adulthood. Alternatively, you can buy a yearling emu pair, but there's no guarantee the two will bond (and if they don't bond, they won't produce eggs).

By the age of two, emus are full grown and able to reproduce, although two-year-old pairs won't be proven breeders. If you aren't the risky type, you can buy more expensive "proven" breeding pairs, which are guaranteed to produce eggs. November through March is the typical egg-laying period, and a happy emu will lay every three or four days, producing between 25 and 30 eggs a season. Superior layers can produce up to 50. If you decide to let the eggs hatch out instead of making them into a giant omelet, it will take an average of about 52 days to hatch, depending on the air temperature.

Emus are popular as livestock animals because they don't require much space (just 2,000 to 3,000 square feet per breeding pair), they're extraordinarily healthy, and they're happy to eat commercial ratite

Neil Williams, emu farmer

Neil Williams comes from a long line of Tennessee farmers—both his father and his father's father before him raised cattle, hogs, and chickens. So when Neil was ready to retire from his job as an IBM salesman back in 1992, he and his wife Lois figured they'd like to buy some land and raise animals. "It was kind of by accident," he recalls. "I just stumbled upon emus." Some other farmers in his area had the birds, and so he and Lois started traveling to different shows and conventions to research the value of the bird.

Convinced there was a living to be had raising emus, they bought about eight proven breeders and set up shop at their Fun-Knee Farm. When they started, most farmers primarily raised and sold just the birds, but it soon became evident that to survive farmers would need to branch out into emu products as well. "To survive in the emu industry, you pretty much have to be a farm-to-finish business," Williams says. "You have to do it all yourself."

Recognizing the trend, Neil and Lois established Back Country Emus to sell the products their birds produced, including emu oil, eggs, oil products, and some leather products. Although they sell incubated eggs to others interested in hatching emus, they also do a rousing business in selling egg shells.

They also sell emu meat, which they send to USDA-inspected professionals to process. Very similar to beef, emu meat is very low in fat and extremely low in cholesterol, and comes in a wide variety of styles: tenderized steaks, roast, ground meat, summer sausage, breakfast sausage, Polish sausage, jerky, and hot dogs.

"I guess we like the benefit we give to our customers and to ourselves," Williams says. "We use emu products ourselves, for our own aches and pains … we're a walking testimony to emus." The family eats three or four pounds of the heart-healthy meat a week. "It's the only red meat that's listed as heart healthy on the Web site of the American Heart Association," he says. "We have a couple of hospitals in Nashville that send their heart patients to us—emu meat is the only red meat they recommend." Both Neil and Lois also swear by the usefulness of their emu

(continues)

chow in mash or pellet form. They're also typically gentle creatures that aren't aggressive toward humans. However, if you corner an emu against a wall, its instinct will be to try to push past you—and a kicking or struggling emu has injured inexperienced farmers. More typically, an adult used to humans can be handled by being gently guided by its wings.

If you're interested in emus, you've also got to decide what markets are available for the eggs, oil, meat, leather, or feathers your birds produce. You can make a high-quality leather from emu hides, which is thinner and of a finer texture than leather from ostrich. It's used to produce a wide range of accessories, clothing, and boots.

Emu meat is a heart-healthy choice, as it's lower in cholesterol and higher in protein than beef or pork. With a fat content about the same as chicken or turkey, emu can be purchased as steaks, sausage, jerky, or ground meat. You can get about 26 pounds of meat per emu.

(continued)

oil for their arthritis, both topically and internally. Lois has been able to wean herself off all her arthritic medications for the past nine years, Neil says, because of the emu oil she takes instead.

The two keep about 250 birds on their acre farm. "We've scaled back, because it's hard to run a business and handle the farm at the same time," Williams says. Although emus are "easy keepers," they stand up to six feet tall and can jump traditional fences, so the Williams have enclosed the emu paddocks with special six-foot fences. "They do run fairly fast," Williams observes, "and once they get outside, they can be 10 miles away in nothing flat. In our part of the country we have coyotes and other predators, so it's dangerous for the emu to escape."

A typical day depends on the time of year. "Today we're in the middle of egg-laying season, from November through March," he says. "We gather the eggs every day, and if I have a hatching contract or a reason to hatch, I'll store the eggs until we have enough to hatch." Emu eggs can be stored for up to 30 days, but if Williams isn't going to hatch them, he drains the eggs and sells the eggshells as craft pieces all over the world. Emu eggs are a dark avocado green, with several different layers of color in the shell from green to white. Engraving on the shell results in a beautiful variety of colors.

Emu eggs are also edible, but since one egg is equal to about eight chicken eggs, you have to be a real egg-hungry family in order to crack one open. Although there are no health advantages to emu eggs, they are light and airy, and taste identical to a chicken egg. "Sometimes we take a hard boiled egg along for a conversation piece," Neil laughs.

"Our business has grown every year," he says. "The first five or six years were a bird business, with just buying and selling birds. That worked its way through a cycle, until everybody who wanted a bird had one, and the demand for birds became nonexistent. Those of us who believed in what the bird represented started doing research, and we developed products."

Even more popular is emu oil, which is rendered and refined from emu fat. Emu oil has been used for hypoallergenic skin care, in cosmetics, and as an anti-inflammatory for years. Emu oil proponents swear it can lessen wrinkles and soften the skin better than Botox—without the risks or injections. This highly marketable oil is currently being produced by many beauty and cosmetic companies, and is used by many national sports teams to help reduce inflammation and soreness in muscles and joints. Since 1995, the emu oil business in the United States has really taken off, increasing by more than 300 percent. Today, there are more than 1,000 emu oil products sold in department stores, pharmacies, and health food stores in the United States and around the world. You can even drink the stuff, and proponents swear it helps reduce acid reflux and arthritic inflammation. Although several University of Massachusetts studies of emu oil have proven its benefits in animals, funding has not yet been available to test these products in humans.

Emu eggshells are highly prized as craft materials, and there's even a use for the beautifully fluffy feathers, which are popular in the fashion world for their unique appearance. These feathers are also used to plump out feather dusters.

Pitfalls

As with any animal-related agriculture job, raising emus can be confining because you can't just take off and go on vacation without providing backup help for the animals. And although emus are generally docile, if they're crowded they can kick, inadvertently hurting inexperienced handlers.

Perks

If you love animals and can't think of anything you'd rather do than spend your time working with emus, this job offers independence, flexibility, and the ability to work for yourself and be close to nature.

Get a Jump on the Job

Since there are emu farms in all 50 states, you probably have access to these birds without having to drive too far. The best way to find out if you have a knack for emu farming is to jump right in and see, so contact a local emu farmer or the American Emu Association for information. See if you can get an after-school or summer job helping around the emu farm—or even offer to work for free, just to get some experience and see if emus are the critters for you. Some state 4-H programs also offer emu projects for their members.

FISH FARMER

OVERVIEW

Not all fishermen make a living on a small boat tossed about on the high sea—some fishermen make a living right in their own backyards. Fish farmers breed and raise fish and shellfish in fresh or saltwater tanks, ponds, or cages, raising fish for the food industry, to stock ponds, and sometimes to sell as ornamental fish. Some fish farmers raise fish in ponds and then charge people to come and catch the fish. You'll find a wide variety of fish nurtured via aquaculture, including catfish, trout, tilapia, salmon, shrimp, and mussels. Largemouth bass, trout, and bluegill are commonly raised for stocking purposes.

Aquaculture was first developed in China about 3,500 years ago. In the United States, however, fish farming was not a common way to make a living because wild fish were so readily available. Sadly, overfishing has resulted in the harvest of fewer wild fish, while the demand for fish and shellfish continues to increase. Fish farming fills an agricultural niche, and the number of fish farms is expected to increase.

There's a lot to learn about fish farming, which is why it's so important to get adequate education and training. If you become a fish farmer, you may breed fish from eggs, or buy small fish to raise. (It's easier to start with small fish, but they're more expensive than eggs.) While fish are raised in tanks, ponds, or cages, shellfish are farmed in their natural environment (for example, mussels are cultivated on ropes that hang into the sea).

AT A GLANCE

Salary Range

Income fluctuates widely, both within the industry and from year to year, depending on conditions and factors that affect the quantity and quality of crop. If you work for a fish farmer, you might expect to earn about $20,000 a year to start. Housing sometimes is provided.

Education/Experience

Should have high school training that includes courses in math, biology, and other life sciences, and preferably, a two- or four-year degree in agriculture, marine biology, or a related field. Formal programs are available that address topics such as hydrology, hatchery management and maintenance, fish culture, and fisheries biology.

Personal Attributes

You should have a true interest in fish, enjoy working outside, be reasonably physically fit, enjoy working around water, and be able to swim. You also will need to be able to work on your own or as part of a small team, and have good communication and organizational skills.

Requirements

Any type of farming requires a great deal of knowledge in many areas. In addition to agricultural skills, you'll need managerial skills in order to keep the farm running. Knowing how to maintain equipment is a plus, and you'll need a good understanding of water quality, chemicals used in fish farming, and so forth.

Outlook

Although farm employment in general is expected to continue to decline, aquaculture, or fish farming, is on the rise and should continue to provide employment opportunities through 2012.

One of the most important jobs you'll have as a fish farmer is to understand and be able to maintain water quality. Healthy fish can't grow in unhealthy water, and you risk disease and infection among your fish if water quality deteriorates. This has been a concern with farm-raised salmon, which are raised in close quarters and grow to be very large.

You can't expect fish to survive on their own in a tank, which means you've got to feed them, either by hand or using automatic feeders. Once they've reached the right size, it's time for harvesting—but exactly how this is done depends on what they'll be used for. Those to be used for stocking and ornamental purposes must

be carefully transported, while those that have been raised for food are killed, cleaned, packed in ice, and then transported. Some types of fish to be used for food are transported live to markets.

Raising and harvesting fish, however, is only part of the job for a fish farmer. You've also got to have good managerial skills to keep a farm working and making money. There are financial issues, safety regulations, and changing farming techniques to keep up with. Farmers sometimes are eligible for governmental agricultural support programs, but you need to know how to go about applying for funds.

Jim Bradley, fish farmer

Jim Bradley's family has farmed the area around Ladoga, Indiana, for more than 80 years. None of his ancestors, however, could have guessed that in 1988 Bradley would trade in his cattle, hogs, and grain to raise a tropical fish called tilapia.

"I was looking for something with a future, something I could support my family with, and the kind of farming I was doing didn't look all that bright," Bradley says. "I'd read an article about aquaculture that a professor at Purdue University had written, and I thought it seemed like something I could do."

After reading some more and doing a lot of thinking and planning, Bradley enlisted the help of his son to build a dozen 6,400-gallon rectangular tanks, each of which holds about 5,000 pounds of fish. The tanks are kept indoors in a controlled environment.

The rest, as they say, is history. One of the first to raise fish in the Midwest, Bradley is now, in addition to running his aquaculture business, helping other farmers get started in fish farming. When he first set up shop, there was little equipment available for fish farmers. He adapted what was available and came up with his own designs for fish tanks, filtration systems, and so forth. Bradley has become something of a specialist in aquaculture equipment, and enjoys helping others get set up and started in their own businesses. He recently started a company called Aqua-Manna to assist fledgling fish farmers.

That's not to say, however, that he's not actively raising fish himself. In fact, after three failed attempts, he recently raised his first crop of shrimp.

"I killed the first three batches of shrimp, but I raised this last one," Bradley says.

It takes about four months to raise shrimp from their larvae stage to be ready to eat. The wait, Bradley notes, was worth it. "They were excellent tasting shrimp," he says. "And we don't use any preservatives or chemicals or hormones of any sort. They're raised in well water and given natural feed. That's it."

(continues)

You'll also need to be able to manage employees, keep financial records, and be able to communicate well with customers and potential customers. Knowing how to market your product also is very important. Along with a growing demand for farm-raised fish is an increasing number of fish farms, meaning there will be more competition when you're looking for customers.

Pitfalls

As with any type of farming, fish farming requires a seven-day week, with lots of hard work. Fish need to be fed and tended to every day, meaning if you want to go away or take a day off, you've got to get someone lined up to do the chores for you.

Perks

If you have a real interest in fish, dream of being your own boss, and you aren't afraid of hard work, fish farming provides many opportunities and is sure to be an interesting career.

Get a Jump on the Job

In addition to the appropriate education, the best way to get a jump on being a fish farmer is to get a job on a fish farm, either as a farm hand or an apprentice. Some farms may offer internships. Meanwhile, you can read all about fish farming and start to think about what sort of operation you might be interested in running and what sort of fish you might raise.

(continued)

The same is true with the tilapia, which is Bradley's main crop. He raises between 50,000 and 120,000 pounds of fish each year, growing them in seven to nine months from tiny fry (they start out about a half-inch long and weighing about half a gram) to an average weight of a pound and a quarter. He sells them in markets and restaurants in Cleveland, St. Louis, Kansas City, Chicago, and other cities, often delivering them live.

"A lot of people like to get them when they're alive," Bradley says. "That way they know that they're really fresh, and I can tell them about how they've been raised. People like to know where their fish comes from."

The greatest challenge to American aquaculture is competition from countries such as Vietnam, Thailand, and India. Fish farmers in those countries raise and sell fish and shrimp at prices with which American farmers can't compete. "Filets come in from these places and sell for $1.24 per pound," Bradley says. "I can't raise a fish for that price."

To be successful, studying up on aquaculture is imperative. "Learning how to market your product is the most important thing," he says. "It's really not that hard to raise the fish. But it's not only raising them, you've got to be able to get rid of them, too. So, you'd better get good at marketing."

Although Bradley has no special training in aquaculture, he's become extremely knowledgeable about it from reading, experimenting, and talking to other fish farmers. He's worked with university researchers who are looking to come up with better ways to raise fish, and keeps up with advances and innovations in the field.

"I don't think you ever learn it all," Bradley says. "There's probably always something you can do to make your operation better and more efficient."

FORESTRY CONSULTANT

OVERVIEW

If your hero is more the Johnny Appleseed type than the Paul Bunyan sort, you may want to consider a job as a forestry consultant—a private forester, not employed by the government. Forestry consultants handle a variety of jobs, such as determining boundaries, writing forest management plans, planting trees, managing invasive growth, determining legal issues relating to forestry, and selling timber.

A forestry consultant may work for private landowners, municipalities, or governmental agencies. Unlike a forester who works for the government, private foresters need to find their own clients. They'll also need to have contacts who can help them fulfill the needs of their clients. For instance, if you're hired to plant trees, you'll need to work with a reputable nursery to obtain the type and number of trees your client requires. If you're working to determine boundaries, you may require the services of a surveyor. It's extremely important to have reliable contacts, because their work will reflect on your work and could affect your reputation and your business.

As a forestry consultant, your job is to provide a service or solve a problem concerning an area of forestry. You'll meet with a client to determine his or her needs, then determine what must be done to meet those needs. You'll need to present a plan to your client of how you expect to

AT A GLANCE

Salary Range

Between $30,000 and $50,000 a year, depending on the type of consulting work you do, the area in which you live, and the clients for whom you work.

Education/Experience

You should have a sound knowledge of forest management and an understanding of topics relating to forestry, such as boundary issues, timber, herbicides, tree plantings, forestry regulations and legal issues, and so forth. In states that don't require particular experience in order to be a forestry consultant, you'll probably be more successful if you have a two-year degree as a forestry technician or a four-year bachelor's degree in forestry.

Personal Attributes

You should enjoy being outdoors and be willing to be outdoors in all kinds of weather. You'll need to be in good physical condition to work in forestry. And because you'll work closely with your clients—often on an ongoing basis over a period of time—you'll need to be personable and have good communication skills. You'll also need to be able to organize your time in order to get your work done as scheduled.

Requirements

Some states require foresters to be licensed and/or registered, which may require a particular level of education.

Outlook

Forestry and conservation jobs in general are expected to grow more slowly than average. However, private farm owners recently were offered government incentives to convert all or part of their properties to forest to provide ecological benefits. This sort of land conversion could result in more jobs for foresters and conservation workers.

proceed with the job; an estimate of time and cost for the job; and a contract specifying specific work that the job entails, costs, payment terms, and other pertinent information.

If you're a consultant employed by a company, the company probably will provide help with the business aspects of your jobs. If you have your own consulting company, however, you'll need to take care of contracts and other legal matters on your own.

As you can see, there's more to being a forestry consultant than performing forestry work. That's why it's important to have some business skills, or to know someone who can help you with contracts and other business matters. It's very important to operate professionally when you're working with clients. A business consultant or lawyer could help you draw up a contract to use, or you could consult the U.S. Small Business Administration (http://www.sba.gov), an organization

Rob Wawrousek, forestry consultant

Rob Wawrousek is a forestry consultant who specializes in timber management. Specifically, he works with clients who, for one reason or another, want to harvest and sell timber from their properties. It may be to make room for a building project, or because the woodland has become overcrowded to the point where the excessive growth is affecting the health of the trees. Or a property owner might simply want to sell valuable wood for the financial benefits.

Keeping woodlands managed and maintained is beneficial to the overall health of a forest, Wawrousek said. "A woodland is just like any other natural entity," he explains. "There are only so many resources available that are necessary in maintaining trees. Trees need water, sunlight, and nutrients from the soil. When those things aren't sufficiently available, the trees suffer."

When Wawrousek gets a call from a prospective client, he sets up an appointment to meet at the property. During that meeting, the client outlines the project, and—based on his forestry and conservation experience—Wawrousek advises the prospective client as to how many and which trees should be harvested.

"There are a lot of people we meet who could care less about forest management," Wawrousek says. "They just want to cut down trees. Our main emphasis is trying to educate people about what is correct from a forestry aspect."

Once Wawrousek and the client have agreed to work together, he establishes property boundaries and marks the trees that are to be harvested. Each tree has to be measured and the type of tree noted. "Basically, we get an inventory of everything that will be taken down," Wawrousek says.

The most common types of wood he sells include different varieties of oak, poplar, ash, birch, and maple. However, he normally can find a buyer for almost any type of wood.

Based on the variety and number of trees to be harvested, Wawrousek formulates an estimate of the value of the trees and presents it in a report to the property owner. He then solicits bids from people and companies who buy wood, including sawmills, timber buyers, and loggers. Generally, he seeks bids from about 45 individuals and companies.

While waiting for the bids to come back, Wawrousek sets up a contract with the landowner for the sale of the timber. The contract includes the safety practices that will be employed when

that provides information and services to owners of small businesses.

Pitfalls

Working as a consultant is not for everyone. It requires the ability to manage your own time, in addition to having a fair amount of business acumen. And working on your own as a consultant means that you need to be able to manage and balance busy times with not-so-busy times, taking into account your finances, family or social life, and other matters that may be affected. If you've studied forestry because you love nature and want to work outside, you might find the business end of your business to be a bit taxing.

Perks

If you love nature and being outside, there's probably no better job for you than a forestry consultant. As a consultant,

cutting the timber, any environmental concerns, the time frame in which the timber will be harvested, the estimated value of the timber, and so forth.

Wawrousek then hires loggers to harvest the timber, overseeing the job as it progresses. Generally, it takes a week to cut between five and seven acres of woodland. The average-sized property that Wawrousek deals with is 70 acres, although he's been involved with projects on as little as 10 acres. Because it takes time to cut wood, and harvesters may not be available to begin cutting for some time after Wawrousek contacts them, he extends all his contracts over an 18-month period.

If someone wants timber on his property cut and sold very quickly, Wawrousek can accommodate the client, but the property owner probably won't do as well financially from the sale of the lumber because Wawrousek won't be able to be as discriminating about who buys it.

Wawrousek has both a two-year degree as a forestry technician and a four-year bachelor's degree in forestry. While he explains that people probably could go into forestry consulting without any formal education, they'll have a much easier time if they have some credentials. Some states require education. "You need that boost—that little piece of paper that's a degree to open doors for you," he says.

Wawrousek thoroughly enjoys his work as a forestry consultant, both for the opportunity to meet and work with interesting clients and the chance to spend a lot of time outdoors. He also likes being involved with conservation efforts and knowing that he's working to maintain healthy woodlands.

He warns, however, that working in the woods is different than being in the woods for recreational purposes. "Working in the woods is a lot different from playing in the woods," Wawrousek says. "Just think about when it's 95 degrees and really humid, and you're out there measuring and marking trees, getting stuck on briars and stung by mosquitoes. I tell people it's not all fun and games."

There also are hazards such as snakes and ticks. Still, Wawrousek said he wouldn't change it. "I get a lot of pleasure and satisfaction from what I do," he said. "It's a very satisfying area of work."

your time tends to be more flexible than working set hours for an employer, allowing you to manage your schedule to suit your needs.

Get a Jump on the Job

Some national, state, and local forests and wildlife refuges offer internships for students studying forestry, conservation, or a related field. An internship would provide great learning opportunities and practical experience. Contact your state's natural resources department to find out about possible opportunities. Some cities offer urban forestry internships, and most colleges with forestry programs have internship opportunities for students.

GAME BIRD PRODUCER AND HUNT ORGANIZER

OVERVIEW

If you've ever had a pheasant burst out of the undergrowth in front of you as you traipsed through a meadow or cornfield, you'll understand the thrill associated with game birds. Hunters and nature enthusiasts have long admired the beauty of pheasants, quail, and partridges, as well as their agility and speed. But wild game birds are becoming scarce in many areas of the country, where encroaching development has destroyed their habitats and made them easy prey for predators.

To fill the void for hunters and those who value game birds for their meat, more and more farmers are turning to the cultivation of wild birds to boost their farm income: Chukar partridges, gray partridges, ringneck pheasants, bobwhite quail, Japanese quail, Pharaoh quail, and Red Carneua, White King, and Mondain pigeons. Often, those who raise the birds have enough land that they can offer guided hunts for sportsmen and women who are willing to pay for a chance to bag some birds.

However, because some people are more interested in serving game birds as a gourmet treat rather than shooting at them, game bird producers also typically offer the birds for sale as food. Dressed game birds may be sold directly from the farm, or they might be marketed through grocery stores or specialty shops. Game bird eggs are still another commodity some game bird producers have discovered.

While raising birds and organizing hunts might sound like fun, it involves lots

---

AT A GLANCE

Salary Range

Salary varies greatly, depending on the scope of the operation, how and to whom the birds are sold, the type of hunts offered, and so forth. Many people who raise game birds have at least one additional source of income. The average salary range for game bird farmers and farm managers is between $32,000 and $59,000, according to government figures.

Education/Experience

Raising game birds requires advanced knowledge about birds and their habitats. A degree in animal science is preferred and highly recommended.

Personal Attributes

Must be tenacious, willing to put in long hours (sometimes in addition to another job), and willing to take risks. You'll also need a fairly good level of physical endurance, especially if you plan to lead hunts. Good business and organizational skills also are important.

Requirements

Depending on how large an operation you wish to run, you'll need a sizeable tract of property to accommodate the birds. Because of differing zoning restrictions and land use regulations, you'll need to make sure you have the proper permits from your municipality.

Outlook

Although farm employment in general is expected to continue to decline, niche operations such as raising game birds and organizing hunts are expected to fare well as people search for gourmet food items and new recreational opportunities.

---

of work and a significant investment. Game birds, depending on the type and how many you buy, can be pretty pricey (between two and three dollars each for baby ringneck pheasants, for instance), and there is a lot of equipment you need at first to get started in the business. You risk losing a significant investment if your flock fails to prosper.

Andrew Slaugh, game bird producer and hunt organizer

Andrew Slaugh has been raising ringneck pheasants and Chuckar quail for four years now on his Sycamore Hollow Farm in Lancaster, Pennsylvania. In conjunction with raising the birds, he offers bird hunts on property near his farm. Slaugh also raises Angus cattle and sells the meat, and operates a small carpentry business.

He got into the game-bird business because he'd always enjoyed hunting pheasant and quail, and figured that there'd be a need for people to raise birds in order to assure there would be adequate numbers for sportsmen and women.

"I remember when you didn't have to buy pheasants, they were all over the place," Slaugh says. "But between farming and development, we've taken away their cover. The predators had a field day and the numbers of birds are significantly reduced."

Anticipating the need, he studied up on game bird production, and as they say, the rest was history.

Slaugh buys 1,500 birds at one time, on the same day they're hatched. "I buy the whole flock at once," he says. The birds are initially put into two heated rooms, each twelve-by-twelve feet, and kept at 105 degrees. After about a month, Slaugh opens up the area to create a flyway for the young birds, and puts a device over their beaks that prevents them from pecking each other. "They're pretty nasty birds," Slaugh says. "Without those things they'd be fighting all the time."

About seven weeks after he brings them home, Slaugh moves the birds out to an acre of land, where they are contained with netting. The area is planted with corn and thick weeds to provide food and cover for the birds, and Slaugh makes sure they have an adequate water supply.

When the birds are about 18 weeks old, they're fully grown and feathered, and can be used for the hunts. Slaugh offers three-hour morning and afternoon hunts six days a week. Hunters can opt for four, seven, or twelve birds, which Slaugh releases before the hunt begins. Most hunters, he says, usually shoot about three-quarters of the released birds. For additional fees, Slaugh will smoke them or prepare the birds for cooking.

Although Slaugh enjoys raising the birds and organizing the hunts, he admits it's not an easy way to make money. While he sells some of the birds to a neighboring farm zoned for conservation, most of his game bird–related income comes from the hunts.

"I think unless you have the ground to do the hunts, raising birds probably isn't a great idea," he says. Slaugh has a degree in animal science, and he uses his knowledge in raising game birds and developing feeds for the cattle. He recommends that anyone interested in raising animals commercially get a degree, or at least adequate training.

"It's work, and you've got to know what you're doing," Slaugh says. "I've always enjoyed hunting game birds and I was looking at a way to make some money from it. But I couldn't have done it if I hadn't had the background in animal science. I wouldn't have had the expertise."

Many game bird producers raise pheasants—one of the most popular breeds raised as game birds, which can be obtained hatched or unhatched. If you buy eggs, you'll need incubators in which to hatch them and a heat room for the newly hatched pheasant chicks. After about four weeks, most of the birds are ready to leave the heated area and move to a place where they'll learn to fly. At this point, guards are installed over their beaks to prevent them from pecking each other—sometimes to death.

When the pheasants are about seven weeks old, they can be moved to a controlled area outdoors. Ideally, the area in which they're contained will be under net, and heavily planted with corn and other cover. It doesn't take the birds long to knock down everything that's planted, making it necessary to have enough land to relocate them until the original patch of land regenerates.

Because birds are susceptible to certain viruses and other diseases, great care must be taken in order to maintain a healthy flock. If birds are to be added to the flock, they should be quarantined for a time first to make sure they are healthy. And, of course, if you're going to use the birds in hunts, you need to have a property suitable for that use.

Raising game birds can be profitable, but you'll need to have some pretty serious business savvy to successfully market your business. There are different directions in which you can go, so you'll need to determine which route makes the most sense for you.

If you don't have property suitable for hunting, for instance, you might concentrate on marketing the birds as a gourmet food product or use them for egg production. Or you could collaborate with someone who does have property suitable for hunting to provide birds for hunts there.

You also need to be sure that you have the necessary equipment to successfully raise birds, and that you raise them appropriately for their intended use. Birds marketed as food, for instance, are fed differently than those being raised for hunts.

Pitfalls

You'll need to come up with a significant amount of money to get started in the game-bird business, and there are no guarantees that you'll be wildly successful. Game birds can be temperamental and require close tending. As with any type of farming, the work of raising birds is ongoing and constant.

Perks

Raising animals is fun, and if you enjoy being outdoors and working with birds, you'll have a good time as a game bird farmer. You also may be eligible for tax breaks if your land is used as farmland.

Get a Jump on the Job

Start by learning everything you can about different kinds of game birds and how to raise them. If you know of a game bird farm in your area, ask the farmer if you can help out with the birds. That will give you a chance to observe the birds and see how they're cared for. Some youth agricultural programs, such as 4-H youth educational programs, can offer information about game birds, and may assist you in raising a few birds.

GAME WARDEN

OVERVIEW

When you say "game warden," most people think of the guy who comes around checking for fishing licenses when you're out on the lake. What many people don't realize is that game wardens are also involved across North America in fighting forest fires, performing avalanche control, capturing and relocating wildlife, and handling remote search-and-rescue operations. They also may patrol international borders and prosecute the organized wildlife black market. Wardens watch over parks, forests, waterways, migratory paths, federal and tribal lands, and military bases, and they may need to patrol thousands of miles of rugged backcountry.

Game wardens are licensed peace officers. Similar to other types of police, fish and game warden positions are based on military rank. If you're interested in being a game warden, you'll start out as a cadet, move up to lieutenant, and then to captain. Some agencies may require you to take exams for advancement or supervisory positions, or you may move up in the ranks by taking positions in other states.

Game wardens enforce the laws that protect wildlife, and they also keep track of wildlife populations, making sure there aren't too many or too few of each type of animal. Wardens gather data through research and observation. If they find an irregularity in the number of animals, they try to correct the problem. If the number of animals is low, wardens recommend

AT A GLANCE

Salary Range

Nationally, the median wage for fish and game wardens is $3,420 per month ($19.72 per hour). Half of all fish and game wardens earn between $2,710 and $4,200 per month ($15.64 and $24.24 per hour). Fish and game wardens are paid extra for working holidays and weekends. Wages increase as workers advance in the government ranking system, and also vary by experience and level of responsibility. Special agents earn more than other wardens. Fish and game wardens usually receive benefits such as paid vacation and sick leave, health insurance, and a retirement plan.

Education/Experience

Most fish and game wardens attend the same law enforcement academy as police patrol officers. Depending on the job, training may run from three months to two years. Those who are wildlife special agents or inspectors generally have more specialized training. Most wardens have a bachelor's degree. Combining a wildlife management major with law enforcement courses is good preparation. Community colleges, technical schools, and universities all offer these courses. Employers prefer to hire applicants who have at least two years of college (they may accept three years of related work experience instead of a degree). Some employers require a master's degree. Many wardens have degrees in biology, criminal justice, or related disciplines, but this is not required. Most fish and game wardens learn their skills through both formal and on-the-job training.

Personal Attributes

Common sense and good people skills are vital; must be willing to enforce laws, be a self-starter, able to work alone or with others, and possess a strong desire to serve hunters, anglers, boaters, and wildlife enthusiasts. Should like to work with plants, animals, and physical materials such as wood, tools,

AT A GLANCE

and machinery, enjoy working outside, and have investigative interests.

Requirements

Applicants may be required to pass a background check and a physical exam; some state agencies may require a physical endurance or agility test. Some states require that fish and game wardens be certified, but requirements vary by state. In general, candidates must be at least 21 years of age, have a valid driver's license, and be in good physical condition. Experience as a law enforcement officer is a good background if you specialize in fish and game law enforcement.

Outlook

Nationally, the number of jobs for fish and game wardens is expected to grow more slowly than average through the year 2012. The number of jobs in this field is related to the amount of money state or federal governments spend on fish and game management. The amount of money depends on what issues are priorities locally or nationally. In addition, funding depends on whether elected officials see wildlife management as an important issue.

changes to protect animals. They may do this by improving the animals' habitat or by changing laws. If there are too many animals, wardens must determine how to thin the population. In addition, wardens must try to figure out if the change in the number of animals is a long-term event or just temporary.

Besides monitoring wildlife, wardens also enforce hunting and fishing laws, checking to make sure hunters and fishers have licenses and aren't taking too many animals. If somebody breaks the law, a game warden can write a ticket or even arrest an offender. They also may seize the person's gear or their catch, if it was taken illegally. In addition, wardens investigate hunting accidents and may promote hunter safety.

Fish and game wardens frequently work with the public. They may make presentations to schools or sporting clubs about where animals live, how they survive, and what is being done to protect them. They also work with people who live near wildlife areas. Fish and game wardens investigate property or crops that may have been damaged by animals. For example, they may determine whether a sheep was attacked by wolves, coyotes, or dogs. They do this by examining tracks and other evidence. Wardens suggest ways that property owners can prevent future damage. They also record the amount of damage and estimate how much the owners will be paid for their loss.

Game wardens are also called fish and wildlife managers or wildlife officers. Some wardens become wildlife inspectors or special agents. Wildlife inspectors work at major U.S. entry ports to decrease the illegal trade of fish and wildlife. Special agents are trained as criminal investigators. They may work undercover to expose illegal businesses, such as people hunting animals that are at risk of being extinct. Special assignments may include special undercover operations or patrol using jet skis, jet boats, airplanes, horseback, canoes, all-terrain vehicles, and motorcycles.

Many people choose to be a game warden instead of a police officer because new police officers often must spend the first several years of their careers working in a jail environment or in an administrative

Tom Grohol, game warden

Tom Grohol spent much of his childhood outdoors, fishing and prowling through the woods of central Pennsylvania. "The outdoors was an important part of our life," he recalls. As a youngster, Grohol was befriended by their local game warden, who became his mentor. He began taking forestry courses in college, and eventually decided he'd like to become a volunteer deputy game warden after he turned 21.

It was the start of a long trek toward his career goals. "Jobs in this field aren't easy to come by," he notes, "and competition is very keen." There just aren't that many game wardens in Pennsylvania. He volunteered as a part-time officer for a number of years while taking law enforcement courses at night. Then he started taking the Civil Service exams—again and again. "It took me 10 years to get a full-time position," he says. "I tried four times before I was accepted into the game commission's training academy."

After completing the one-year residential academy program, he was given his first district. "When you sign on, you agree you can be put anywhere in state. I was assigned to Lancaster County." He worked for 10 years as field officer, volunteering for special assignments at the training academy. Three years ago he was promoted to his current position as chief of the administrative division in the Pennsylvania Game Commission's Bureau of Law Enforcement.

Right away, he loved the job. Working from his home office, he was responsible for every scrap of wildlife in the entire area. A big part of the job involves public relations—teaching wildlife programs for schools, civic organizations, and sportsman's clubs, and teaching hunter-trapper courses. He was also responsible for wildlife management, conducting wildlife surveys to help biologists. Then there was the law enforcement part of the job, enforcing the game and wildlife code—especially during hunting season—by checking for licenses, guarding against violations, and answering complaints that a hunter was shooting too close to a house or trespassing on private land.

"A lot of people are under the impression that they'll spend all their time out in the woods nursing Bambi back to health," he says. "That couldn't be further from the truth. The job involves lots of office time, paperwork—25 percent of my time was spent in the office. I probably spent less time in the woods than the average person!"

He recommends that young naturalists interested in working as a game warden try to study anything outdoor-related—specifically wildlife management or forestry. "Some colleges have wildlife law enforcement for people who want to be a game warden. At this point there are no education requirements beyond high school, but competition is so keen, people with a college degree are going to do better on tests.

"What with the office in your home, you're always there when the phone rings and it's hard to get away from the job. I'd work almost every weekend because that's when people are outdoors—so your days off are usually during the week. In hunting season days off are few and far between."

The one disadvantage, he thinks, is that while normal police officers have other officers to share the duty, a game warden is basically it. "Whatever happens when you're not working will be on your plate when you come back," he says.

"I liked dealing with the sportsmen; sportsmen are the backbone of what you do. There's also a lot of freedom with the job. You can schedule your own hours. I enjoyed it all."

job. Game wardens are out in the field as soon as they have successfully completed the academy, patrolling the fields and streams and enforcing the law. In addition, wardens have their offices in their homes and enjoy a great deal of flexibility in their schedules. Because wardens work out of their homes, they work independently and do not need to report to a precinct every day for assignments. Wardens are given a patrol area and become the experts on how best to protect the resources in their district. They may patrol assigned areas by car, boat, airplane, horse, or on foot.

Pitfalls

As with any other law enforcement career, being a game warden can be dangerous. Wardens patrol alone, often in remote locations with minimal backup.

Perks

Where else can you combine working with the public, enjoying the outdoors, working with lots of freedom and independence, with enforcing the laws to keep everyone safe and the environment healthy?

Get a Jump on the Job

If you're interested in becoming a game warden, you should take college prep courses, including four years of English, three years of math, three years of social studies, and two years of science. Some colleges also require two years of a second language.

Gaining experience in the field is important while attending college. One way to get experience is a summer job or internship at a national park or fish hatchery, or by working with crews who perform stream or wildlife surveys.

HIKING TRAIL DESIGNER

OVERVIEW

If you've ever hiked along a trail through a national or state park, you might not have given much thought to the finer points of trail design. But you can be sure that someone did—the hiking trail designer. In fact, you'd probably be surprised at how detailed the instructions can be for building a new trail, with details on width, grade, and "sight lines"—the visible upcoming and retreating views that a hiker sees on any part of a trail. If a trail has good sight lines, there will be only a very gradual change in the landscape's colors and textures.

This is no small detail, because how a trail designer chooses to shape the path can affect the hiker's experience. Should the trail angle sharply off in one direction to avoid an obstacle, or should it be gently contoured around a slope? Thoughtfully designed trails allow hikers to encounter wildlife, geography, and geology of the forest or mountain environment. Elevation, soil type, rainfall, and population densities all play an important role in how a trail is built.

In fact, this is no spur-of-the-moment volunteer-type job. Government agencies typically conduct exhaustive environmental studies before they ever allow a designer to stick a shovel into the ground.

When you're building a hiking trail, you don't want it to look brand new, as if someone just hacked her way through the underbrush. A well-designed hiking trail should look as if it's always been there, flowing naturally through the landscape without ever being jarring or seeming arti-

ficial. Indeed, some trail designers practice the Chinese art of *feng shui*—the art of arranging elements to create harmony in color and texture, form and lines.

Pitfalls

Precisely because this job is so desirable, it's a fairly competitive field, with not a lot of jobs to go around.

Perks

This job combines a love and respect of nature with artistic skills and a creative outlet. What could be better for someone

Claudia Wiley, hiking trail designer

Getting paid to go out and hike and look at trails and try to rectify situations, I have to pinch myself!" says Colorado hiking trail designer Claudia Wiley. "It sure beats the heck out of being in the corporate world." As a seasonal trail designer for the Summit County Open Space and Trails, her job is to help design and build woodland trails that make the most of the experience for the hiker while maintaining the environmental integrity of the area.

Wiley started out volunteering as a trail builder, and then went on to take some courses in trail design. "As part of my volunteer work, I learned how to design trails," she explains. "Volunteering has evolved into my seasonal work."

When she's designing a trail, Wiley takes into account a number of factors, including the terrain, where the trail starts and stops, and what features or contours you want to emphasize along the way. "You have to think about where you want to have people go," Wiley says. "Maybe there's a scenic overlook, or places you'd want them to avoid, such as walking through wetlands." She also tries to design a trail that follows the contours of the land, without going straight up and down, which would create erosion.

"You also have to take into account what water does to a trail, because water is the enemy of trails." To do this, she must figure where water crosses a trail, how water could damage the area, and move a trail above a wet boggy area. You even need to take into consideration late snowfall, where water would be staying on a trail and people would begin to walk around a wet area. "When that happens," Wiley says, "What started out as a three-foot trail is suddenly 20 feet wide."

Wiley also considers trail users and type of trail—is it just a hiking trail, or does it have multiple uses, for mountain bikes, horses, and hikers? "All these have to be built somewhat differently based on the population who uses it."

(continues)

who loves hiking, nature, and being outdoors? Many nature enthusiasts consider designing hiking trails to be one of the most satisfying ways to earn a living.

Get a Jump on the Job

The very best way to learn about how to design trails is to volunteer during the summer with a national organization that offers summer "volunteer vacation" opportunities in trail building. Any state—especially those with one of the national premier trails, such as the Colorado Trail in the West, Appalachian Trail in the East, and the Continental Divide Trail—has trail organizations that offer the opportunity to do trail work. This will help you learn how to properly build trails, and what to look for when building trails. Ask questions of crew leaders and volunteer directors. Pick their brains about trail building to help you understand why trails are designed in certain ways. Check out the American Hiking Society for more information as well.

(continued)

First, Wiley goes out in an area where a trail is going to be, to get a sense of the trail's layout. "That's where you start figuring out control points, starting, stopping." Then she puts in a flag line by hanging flagging tape on trees, just to see whether the general area is going to work.

The second step is to actually "shoot the trail" with an instrument that measures the percentage of grade. "Sometimes what feels comfortable for a trail designer isn't so comfortable for the hiker," she notes. "I'm used to hiking on steeper trails, but we try to design no more than a 7 percent grade." If a trail is going to be too steep, the designer may have to include turns or switchbacks just to help the hiker get from point A to point B and still have a hikeable elevation gain.

"After that second go-round is when I start breaking [it] down into workable 100-foot sections," Wiley says, "and I start writing down the type of work that needs to be accomplished." Does the trail call for basic trail work? A rock step? A switchback or a climbing turn?

Designing a trail correctly necessitates at minimum three site visits or trips to the trail, plus usually a fourth one to make sure measurements are correct. "I usually use a 100-foot measuring wheel that measures by inches. On this fourth trip, I write notes—it's kind of a tweaking stage."

Wiley has been designing trails for four years and building them for 13. "Designing a trail gives me a sense of accomplishment," she says. She loves designing a trail and watching hikers use it. "I get a sense of accomplishment when they come off a trail and say 'That's a great trail! I'll never look at a trail the same way.'

"Knowing you're doing some good with the environment [is great]—that you're not damaging the trail but people are still able to enjoy the experience of being in the wild. I have worked with youth groups, especially with girls, and at the end of a hard week, they say: 'Wow! I didn't know I would have so much fun doing this.' People take trails so much for granted until you have to fix or build one, and then look at it very differently."

INSECT CONTROL TECHNICIAN

OVERVIEW

Creepy crawly critters send most people fleeing, but some intrepid souls find working with insects to be fascinating. In fact, insect control technicians perform an important service by identifying pests and removing them from homes, businesses, restaurants, hospitals, schools, and other public and private spaces. They also help manage pests in agricultural settings. A good pest control technician has sound knowledge of insects and the methods and chemicals used to control them, and some of the best insect control operators have degrees in entomology, which is the study of insects.

Controlling insects and other pests requires ingenuity, resourcefulness, and the ability to think through problems and react appropriately. If the idea of taking care of a nest of swarming yellow jackets doesn't make your blood run cold, this could be the job for you. You're likely to encounter situations that are potentially hazardous, and you must be able to remain calm and focused when addressing these situations.

The job of a pest control technician starts with a phone call from a customer experiencing a problem. Pest control is a hands-on business, and a visit to the home or business of the customer is nearly always necessary. Once at the site of the problem, the technician must assess the situation and be able to recommend a treatment.

AT A GLANCE

Salary Range

The salary for a licensed insect control technician (also known as a pest control operator) ranges from $15,700 to $38,000 a year, with a median salary of $24,800, according to the Bureau of Labor Statistics. Earning opportunities increase if you work your way up in a large pest control firm, or if you're successful in starting your own business.

Education/Experience

Although many insect control operators are trained on the job, it's better to take courses through a university extension program or to study the science of entomology at a college or university. Education will help you to advance in this career and give you options concerning the type of work you want to do.

Personal Attributes

You should be reasonably physically fit and able to move easily, as this job entails crawling into small spaces and climbing ladders. Also, you should be able to assess a problem quickly and accurately and react swiftly to a variety of situations concerning insects and other pests. You should be willing to work outdoors in any type of weather, not be intimidated by insects and other pests, and have good attention to detail.

Requirements

Regulations vary from state to state, but in almost all cases an insect control operator must be licensed and/or certified by the state. There also may be local regulations pertaining to the application of pesticides.

Outlook

The outlook for insect control workers is good, with an expected 17 percent increase in jobs through 2012.

This means that you must be able to identify the pests involved, and draw a reasonable conclusion concerning the factors that are bringing them into the home or business. It also requires you to know when pesticides are appropriate, and when the situation may be able to be resolved without pesticides.

As an insect control technician, you'll use different methods to control pests. Getting rid of an insect problem might entail removing a nest, leaving poisonous baits for the insects to ingest and take back to their nests, using pesticides to kill insects, or cleaning out debris harboring pests (such as piles of leaves that attract ticks, or getting rid of old tires that act as breeding grounds for mosquitoes). The practice of using a variety of methods to control pests, instead of simply relying on chemicals to kill them, is called integrated pest management (IPM), and is rapidly becoming the method of choice.

When you get called out on a job, your first task as an insect control technician is to assess the type and extent of the pest problem. You'll need to look for clues such as chewed wood, droppings, and nests, to determine the type of pest and the size of the infestation. Some pests (such as bed-

Lyle Neal, licensed pest control applicator

Lyle Neal still remembers his very first assignment as an insect control technician, nearly 30 years ago. Working with a 25-year veteran of the pest control company J.C. Ehrlich, Inc., of Reading, Pennsylvania, Neal responded to a call about a roach problem in a city home. "That place was crawling with insects," he says.

Neal has treated hundreds of pest problems since then, and has never regretted his decision to apply for a job as an insect control technician.

"I didn't think at six years old that I was going to be a pest control operator," Neal said. "I was going to be a ball player or a doctor or something like that. But it's been a fascinating career."

Neal enjoys the variety of the job, and notes that no day is exactly the same as another. "You might treat the same pests time and time again, but it's always in a different place for a different reason," Neal said. "It's the kind of job where you need to have some seasoning to fully understand what's going on."

Being able to communicate with customers is crucial, Neal says, and a good dose of psychology doesn't hurt. Pest control requires a degree of sensitivity to customers, who may be upset about having pests in their home or anxious about what type of treatment might be necessary.

"Nobody likes having a pest problem," Neal says. "It means a lot to customers to have somebody they can talk to about the problem and to be assured that the problem can be resolved."

Sometimes, Neal says, figuring out a pest problem isn't easy. A customer, for instance, might call and report bees flying in and out from under the eaves of his house. It's the job of the insect control technician to figure out exactly where the bees are nesting, and their access route in and out of the home. For that reason, it's a good idea for insect control technicians to have some knowledge about building construction and to understand the areas of a building in which insects are likely to nest.

bugs) are quite difficult to get under control, and may require a number of visits, while other pests can be removed quite easily.

Controlling insects is not without hazards, because you come in contact not only with the insects themselves, but also the chemicals used to kill them. Protective suits are normally worn to avoid bites and stings and to protect against the chemicals sometimes used to treat pest problems.

While you may not be required to have any education particular to pest management, it's beneficial to have some knowl-

edge of chemistry and entomology. And if you're inclined to pursue a career in entomology, you could explore jobs such as a regulatory entomologist, who works to prevent harmful pests from getting into this country from other countries in plants, animals, produce, and so forth.

A public health insect control technician works for a local, state, or federal health department, while a military technician supervises pest control efforts at military bases and looks for methods to protect military personnel from insect-related illnesses. A forensic insect control technician

Neal, who has a business degree from the University of South Carolina in Columbia, recommends that someone interested in a career in pest control get at least a two-year degree. Some schools do offer courses in structural pest control, or, you might consider working toward a degree in entomology—the study of insects.

"Having either a two-year or four-year degree would really make you marketable for one of the bigger pest control companies," Neal says. "A degree might not be required, but it certainly would give you an edge on the competition for a job."

At the very least, every commercial pesticide applicator must be licensed, normally by the state agricultural department. Pest control is becoming increasingly professional, Neal says, with expectations rising concerning the degree of education and knowledge on the part of technicians.

"People are starting to recognize that there's a public health component of pest control that often doesn't get much recognition," Neal says. "We're learning more all the time about the links between pest control and the health of the public."

Once you have some time under your belt as a licensed insect control technician with an established company, you might think about opening your own business. If that's the case, you'll need to have business skills, in addition to education in pest control. One option when starting your own business, Neal says, is to consider buying an established company from someone who is leaving the business to retire or start a new career. The downside to that, however, is that you'd need significant capital to start.

The best route to go, Neal says, is to get some experience, and be deliberate about what needs to be done before going out on your own. It's better to delay starting your own business until you have the skills and resources necessary to assure it will be successful.

uses their knowledge of insect behavior and life cycles to help solve crimes, while an agricultural technician works to safeguard crops.

Many insect control operators work for a pest control company, while others go into business for themselves. If you choose the latter route, you'll also need to have excellent organizational skills. It's extremely important to keep up with all regulations concerning pest control, to have adequate insurance from a licensed insurer, and to document all your work. You should never work without having a contract that's been signed by your customer that spells out exactly what procedures you'll use, the types of pesticides you'll use, and the expected result. While insect control is not without challenges, it can be a satisfying career for someone who enjoys taking care of problems.

Pitfalls

Insect control requires a lot of attention to detail, and close vigilance paid to mate-rials and techniques used. There is a fair amount of potential liability involved in pest control, and the best way to deal with it is to avoid it by being extremely careful and accountable—all the time.

Perks

If you enjoy solving problems and helping people, you're likely to do well in the area of insect control. Pests in a home or business can be upsetting and detrimental to business, meaning that your efforts to solve the problem are normally much appreciated.

Get a Jump on the Job

Call an insect control company in your area and ask if you can observe the work of its technicians. Read all that you can about the habits of insects, the types of pesticides used to control various pests, and related topics.

IRRIGATION SPECIALIST

OVERVIEW

Water, water, everywhere . . . but how do you get it to the places where there isn't enough? Answer: An irrigation specialist, who might work on a farm, a golf course, or other athletic or recreational facility, in a park, for a municipality, in a large housing development, in a public or private garden—basically any setting where water is an issue.

Irrigation—an artificial method of getting water to land—has been used for centuries. Today's irrigation specialist installs, maintains, operates, and repairs irrigation systems. The person who plans the system is called an irrigation designer, or irrigation design expert. An irrigation specialist, however, may be called upon at times to make minor design adaptations during the course of a job.

As an irrigation specialist, you'll be expected to be able to analyze irrigation problems and come up with solutions to resolve the problems. You'll also need to know how to read the blueprints and specifications that tell you how a system is to be installed, and to understand irrigation hydraulics and pumping systems.

Once the irrigation design specialist has designed an irrigation system for a residential or commercial property, you, as the irrigation specialist, would be expected to implement the design. Working either by hand or with special mechanical equipment, you'd dig trenches in which to lay pipes, install automated controllers that will turn water on and off, install sprinkler heads as specified, and so forth. Installing irrigation systems entails strenuous

AT A GLANCE

Salary Range

The average salary for an irrigation specialist is between $31,000 and $44,000 per year; licensed irrigation specialists with their own business can make much more; in some cases, more than $100,000 a year.

Education/Experience

Experience requirements vary depending on where and for whom you work. To install irrigation systems professionally, you need to be licensed by your state, which requires taking courses through a university extension program or vocational-technical program. You'll be at an advantage if you have a bachelor's, associate's, or vocational-technical degree in grounds management, landscape management, irrigation control, or a related field.

Personal Attributes

A good level of physical fitness is highly recommended, as irrigation work can be physically demanding. You should be able and willing to follow instructions, to communicate ideas, to work effectively with others, and be able to solve problems and come up with solutions to challenges.

Requirements

Irrigation jobs often require that you move from one location to another, so a valid driver's license is usually a requirement to get the job. You'll be required to have knowledge of how manual and automated irrigation systems work, and to understand the principles of irrigation.

Outlook

Good. The gardening and landscape industry is growing, with irrigation work expecting to follow in that trend. The industry is anticipated to grow at a rate of between 10 and 20 percent between now and 2012, making it an attractive area of employment.

physical labor, so it's a good idea to get into shape before taking on the career.

The work of an irrigation specialist who works for a city or other municipality would probably be more varied than one who is employed by a golf course or public garden, for instance. You'd need to have knowledge of any municipal policies and programs relating to irrigation, such as backflow testing and prevention, and you may be called upon to inspect irrigation systems installed for public use by private contractors. Some of the tasks to be performed may require licensing.

Irrigation specialists also must be able to operate some machinery and use a variety of hand and power tools. A background in landscaping is helpful in the irrigation field. Many irrigation systems are computerized, so you'll also need to know about computer applications as they apply to the systems with which you're working.

As if all that isn't enough, you'll also be expected to be able to follow instructions and relate them to others with whom you may be working, to work well with others, to keep track of work you've done and scheduled jobs, to respond to emergency situations, and perhaps to supervise other workers. Generally, the duties of an irrigation specialist are technical and somewhat complex. Some training certainly will be necessary, with either a two- or four-year degree preferred. Some schools offer certification programs for irrigation special-

James S. Tetty, irrigation company owner

James S. Tetty worked in a chemical plant in Houston until about five years ago, when he decided to install an irrigation system in his yard. "I went down to the local hardware store and bought one of those how-to books," he says. "I installed my irrigation system, and the next thing I knew, my neighbors were asking me to put systems in their yards. Pretty soon I was taking time off from my regular job and using my vacations to install irrigation systems for people."

One thing led to another, and after researching the field, Tetty decided to go to school to get certified as a professional irrigation specialist. Already having substantial experience with hydraulics and product movement through piping from his years working in the chemical plant, Tetty was able to get his licenses and certifications as an irrigation specialist and irrigation designer from Texas A&M University in College Station in just 10 weeks. Someone with no or little experience would have to take more courses, which would require a longer time in school, he says. Classes might include water management, backflow protection, irrigation design, hardware, and computer-based irrigation.

Once Tetty was licensed and certified, he began advertising that he was available to design and install irrigation systems, and his new career was launched.

"I've been blessed," Tetty says. "It's going very well. I think that's mainly due to the fact that there aren't too many people in this business in Texas. There are hundreds of thousands of plumbers and electricians, but only 10,000 licensed, certified irrigation specialists in the whole state."

Tetty's company does both residential and commercial work. He recommends that someone just starting out in irrigation work concentrate on residential work, which generally is on a

ists, while others have degree programs in fields related to irrigation.

Pitfalls

Irrigation is vitally important when you're trying to keep a farm, park, or golf course viable, and, if there's a problem with an irrigation system, you'll be expected to drop everything and do something about it immediately. The job also entails a lot of physical work, some of which can be strenuous.

Perks

If you like to be physically active and can't imagine yourself sitting at a desk for eight hours a day, you're likely to enjoy the daily challenges of the job of an irrigation specialist. Every day is likely to be different, and you get to employ creative strategies for solving problems and keeping systems running smoothly.

Get a Jump on the Job

Enroll in your school's vocational-technical education program and begin learning about irrigation through a horticulture or related program. Get a job with a large gardening center, at a golf course, on a farm or in a park where irrigation systems are used, and talk to others who are already working in the field.

smaller scale than commercial. Digging on all residential jobs is done by hand, he said, allowing for a neater looking job.

"People are fussy about their yards in Houston, so we do all the residential work by hand," he says. "We cut out the grass, install the piping, then replace the grass by hand. You can hardly tell we've been there when we're finished."

Tetty thoroughly enjoys his work—both the design aspect and the actual installation of systems. Designing an irrigation system requires thought and planning, he said. Installing a system requires being able to understand and read the design plans, and being able to implement the design. Tetty also maintains and repairs irrigation systems.

While his main focus is irrigation, Tetty spoke of the need to be knowledgeable about marketing and advertising if you plan to run your own business. He advertises aggressively, he said, in the local newspaper, yellow pages, and with brochures. He also has a Web site and makes sure his name and contact information is on all his trucks. "You've got to let people know where you are and what you're selling," Tetty says. "It doesn't matter how good your product or service is if people don't know about it."

Although he doesn't have any formal business training, he recognizes the need to be aware of the business aspects of his company and make sure that operations proceed smoothly. Tetty acknowledges that irrigation work is hard, and he works long hours outside in the hot sun.

"I get asked all the time where I work out," he says. "I tell people I don't work out at all, I just work hard. I guess that's a benefit of irrigation work. You get to play in the dirt and the water, and you get a free workout every day."

LANDSCAPE DESIGNER

OVERVIEW

A landscape designer does exactly what the job title says—designs landscapes. That's a lot more complicated than you might think; you need to know a lot about horticulture and individual plants and their needs, how plants may change over time, a good sense of color and design, and an artistic eye. Landscape designers may work on a simple backyard garden for individual homeowners or magnificent public gardens throughout the country.

The art of designing landscapes is hardly new. People have designed gardens for centuries, and America has had its share of noted historic landscape designers, including Fletcher Steele, Thomas Church, Frederick Law Olmsted, Andrew Jackson Downing, and, of course, Thomas Jefferson. These famous designers fashioned gardens and parks including Central Park in New York City, Longwood Gardens near Philadelphia, Monticello in Virginia, and Naumkeag in Stockbridge, Massachusetts.

Landscape design requires artistic skill and extensive knowledge about plants, soil, drainage, irrigation, building materials, and other topics. It also helps to have good business skills and knowledge of marketing. Artistic and communication skills are important because you need to convey your vision of the design to clients. Although computer programs are capable of handling some design tasks, many landscape designers prefer to sketch all their designs.

AT A GLANCE

Salary Range

Between $40,000 and $55,000 a year for an experienced designer, but the salary can vary greatly depending on location and who you are working for.

Education/Experience

Preferably a bachelor's degree in landscape architecture or a related field, such as botany or design. However, some employers don't require a degree.

Personal Attributes

Must be very creative and able to envision how a space will look and feel, considering light, wind, color, and so forth. Must be able to work well with people and to express yourself effectively. Also should be organized and able to stay on task to complete projects on time. Because landscaping work requires significant physical labor, you should be in reasonably good physical condition.

Requirements

Should have a portfolio showing previous work. Recommendations from former clients are helpful, and you must have sound knowledge of planting and growing requirements for a large variety of plants, shrubs, and trees.

Outlook

Landscape design jobs are expected to grow at a higher than average rate through 2012. The above-average growth is attributed to a growing population requiring new residential, commercial, and other types of construction, and an increasing public demand for beautiful public and private spaces.

An artistic eye isn't the only requirement, however; you won't last long as a landscape designer if you put plants where they won't grow or use species intended for a different type of climate! Plant varieties are constantly changing, so even once

Kellie Carlin, landscape designer

Kellie Carlin worked in the winemaking business in California's famed Napa Valley for 15 years before deciding to hang out her shingle as a landscape designer in St. Helena, California. Landscape design, she says, allows her to incorporate her lifelong love of gardening with her artistic abilities. It also gives the busy mother of three some flexibility with her work schedule.

"I desired the flexibility of working for myself and on my own, on my own schedule. It gives me the luxury at this point of my life to be a mother first and a career woman second."

Carlin is drawn to landscape design because it permits her to work outdoors, and she gets to see her landscape ideas become realities. After her initial meeting with a client, she begins forming images in her mind of how she thinks the design should look. She finds inspiration in books and magazines, incorporating aspects of established design into her ideas.

When she has a pretty good idea of a landscape design that she thinks would work, she begins putting it down on paper so she can convey her ideas to the client.

"I love the planning and the drawing (she does all her drawing by hand) and the idea of helping people realize what will work for them and their lifestyles," she says.

A landscape designer must be very knowledgeable about plants and have the ability to express ideas through words and pictures, but it's also important to be able to work effectively with clients. Sometimes, she says, you think you've come up with a perfect landscape design, only to find out the client doesn't like anything about it. When that happens, you've got to be willing to go back to the drawing board and start again.

"You need to sell yourself and your abilities," she says, "and you need to listen to what the client wants. And you need to be able to sacrifice what you think is appropriate in favor of what they insist they want."

In addition to working well with clients, landscape designers normally work with contractors who build decks and pergolas, install fences, lay pathways, and perform other tasks. Good communication between the landscape designer and the contractor is extremely important.

Carlin is a member of the Association of Professional Landscape Designers, and highly recommends studying horticulture or botany, because a sound knowledge of many varieties of plants and how they grow is necessary. Landscape designers must understand the different qualities of light, different soils, drainage, and irrigation.

"Find a good horticultural program through a community college, or an extension program through a university," she says. "Learn about plants, learn how to draw and memorize botanical names. Learn, learn, learn."

Working for a nursery is a good way to get started in the landscape design business, Carlin advises. Not only will you learn about different plants, you'll meet customers who may, at some point, require the services of a landscape designer. Helping friends with their yards and gardens is another good way to gain experience. And, she says, make sure you start compiling a portfolio early, even if it's just pictures of your own yard to start.

you've learned about specific types, you'll need to keep updating your information.

But that's not all. You can have all the knowledge in the world about plants and related topics, but if you can't market your services or work effectively with clients, you won't be able to be a successful landscape designer. If you're in business for yourself, it's very important to have some business training, as well as horticultural training. You should have a business plan that outlines your goals and how you plan to achieve them. Plus, you'll need to be on top of zoning regulations in the areas in which you'll be working, tax laws, and so forth.

When you're ready to begin designing and implementing landscapes, you'll need to put a marketing plan in place in order to let people know about your business. This also requires some business expertise. Many communities have programs in place, such as SCORE, which matches experienced businesspeople, often retired, with entrepreneurs who are starting their own small businesses. SCORE, a partner with the U.S. Small Business Association, can be found on the Internet at http://www.score.org.

There are many schools that offer horticultural-related programs, and some formal training is highly recommended. Programs available to train you to become a landscape designer include: environmental landscaping, environmental horticultural science, ornamental horticulture, landscape architecture, and garden design. Some schools offer certificate programs, while others have programs for which you'll receive a degree.

Landscape designers often work with contractors who install decks, patios, pergolas, columns, and so forth to support and enhance the landscape design. Be sure to find a contractor with whom you get along and can communicate with effectively. It won't do to have your landscape design ruined because the contractor didn't understand what you wanted.

Pitfalls

There are a lot of established landscape designers, so getting started could be challenging. When the economy weakens, the demand for landscape designs tends to lessen. Outdoor work can be demanding, and you may have to work long hours to complete a job by a specified time. Clients can be demanding and sometimes unreasonable.

Perks

If you love to be outside, have a strong artistic inclination, and enjoy gardening and working with plants and flowers, being a landscape designer is a great job. You get to see an idea take form and become a beautiful reality, and you'll meet some nice and interesting people along the way.

Get a Jump on the Job

Get a job in a nursery in order to expand your knowledge about plants and planting. This also can help you establish contacts with customers who come in looking for advice and information. Offer to build gardens for your friends. Once you do, photograph your work and begin building a portfolio. Check out what kinds of horticultural programs are available at area colleges, community colleges, and university extension services. You also might consider working as an assistant to an established landscape designer or landscape architect.

MAPLE SYRUP PRODUCER

OVERVIEW

Historians don't know exactly how it happened, but at some point some ingenious Native Americans discovered they could obtain sap from a tree and boil it down into a sweet syrup. Legend has it that sap ran out of a gash in a maple tree into a container in which venison was later roasted, reducing the sap to syrup as the venison cooked. Whether or not that story is accurate isn't clear, but somehow, someone along the way discovered the fact that maple sap turns into maple syrup, and men and women have been producing the sweet syrup ever since.

If you're going to make maple syrup as a profession, you've got to be able to read nature's clues in order to know when it's time to begin tapping the maple trees. Tree sap rises with freezing nights and mild days, when the snow melts fast enough to swell creeks, and birds and animals start to move around in preparation for spring.

When you "tap" a maple tree, you drill a small hole into the bark in order to let the sap escape. Some trees can take three or four taps at one time, while others will have only one. Once the tree is tapped, the sap is collected either into a bucket that hangs on the tree and poured into a collection tank, or channeled into a tubing system that carries the sap downhill to the tank. (The tubing system is the modern way of sap collection, and eliminates the need to travel from tree to tree, emptying pails into a collection tank carried on a wagon or truck.)

AT A GLANCE

Salary Range

Varies greatly depending on whether the occupation is full time or part time, conditions affecting harvest, marketing, and other factors. Part-time producers who may have another job and work at making syrup only during March and early April can make several thousand dollars in income, while someone who produces maple syrup and works within the maple industry on a full-time basis can make $50,000 or more.

Education/Experience

No specific degrees are required to be a maple sugar maker, but it helps to have knowledge of topics relating to forestry and agriculture. Some university extension programs offer seminars and workshops dealing with maple syrup production, and some colleges and universities may offer courses relating to the maple industry. Classes or seminars on running a business (especially marketing skills) also would be useful.

Personal Attributes

You should have a good amount of determination, and be willing to work hard and put in long hours during the harvesting season. Attention to detail, the ability to work with others, and a strong drive to succeed are necessary.

Requirements

You must be physically able and reasonably fit to withstand hard work. You also should have the skills necessary to keep track of production, sales, and other business-related aspects of maple syrup production.

Outlook

The demand for maple syrup is increasing while the number of producers is decreasing, meaning that the outlook for maple syrup producers who start or remain in business appears good. While many small farms have consolidated or been purchased by larger ones, others have found niche markets—such as maple syrup related products—that have enabled them to do well.

Weather conditions directly affect sap product: The sap may start running, then stop if it gets colder, and then start again, meaning there's no guarantee that it can be harvested quickly.

Once the sap is harvested, it's placed into an evaporator, which is used to boil down the sap into syrup. If you're the syrup maker, you must keep constant watch, measuring the temperature

Tom McCrumm, maple syrup producer

Tom McCrumm says that maple sugaring isn't an occupation—it's a disease. Once it's in your blood, however, it becomes a passion. McCrumm runs the maple syrup business at South Face Farm in Ashfield, Massachusetts, a small rural and farming community located about 120 miles west of Boston in the foothills of the Berkshire Mountains. In addition to the syrup business, the farm includes a mail-order business and a restaurant featuring foods made with farm-produced syrup.

Although the season for producing maple syrup is short, McCrumm is involved with the industry on a full-time basis. In addition to making syrup and overseeing production at South Face Farm, he consults, sells equipment, and serves as executive director of the Massachusetts Maple Producers Association.

McCrumm has always been fascinated with the business of making maple syrup, but never ceases to be amazed at the amount of work involved and complexity of the business. As with any type of farming, he notes, maple sugaring is weather dependent.

"If the weather is uncooperative, it really affects us," McCrumm says. "A bad week or weather may not have a big effect on field-grown crops or animal farming, but to maple producers, it can mean the difference between a bountiful crop and a disaster of a crop."

On South Face Farm, about 60,000 gallons of maple sap are collected during March and early April and boiled down to produce maple syrup. The trees on the farm are located on a south-facing hillside, providing the ideal opportunity for freezing nights and warm days.

McCrumm says that because the sugaring season is short, you've got to expect to work long, hard days. Branching off into other aspects of the industry such as consulting, mail order, and selling equipment allows him to remain in the maple syrup business all year long, unlike most people, who have supplemental jobs and incomes.

If you're thinking about getting into the business of producing maple syrup, you should study the industry. McCrumm recommends the North American Maple Syrup Producers Manual, which can tell you everything there is to know about the industry, from tree to table. He also advises those interested in maple sugaring to join a state maple producers association and attend meetings, workshops, and tours of sugarhouses.

"Be observant and ask a lot of questions," he advises. "We are a big family of fine folks, always willing to help out someone new."

However, he warned, no matter how long you're in the business, don't ever think that you've learned all there is to know about making syrup and the maple syrup industry. "Maple sugaring is Mother Nature keeping us amused and confused all at the same time," McCrumm says. "You never learn it all, and there are always answers to be found."

to determine the point at which the sap becomes syrup.

After the syrup is made, it must be packaged and sent off to stores and customers around the globe. Then—once the trees stop producing sap and syrup production ends—it's time to clean all the equipment, including spouts, tanks, buckets, and all the tubing used to transport sap.

Some maple producers work full time, year-round, while others make syrup as a way of earning some extra income on the side. Full-time maple producers usually combine seasonal syrup making with year-round packaging, production, and marketing of maple-related products, such as the maple sugar candy you find in specialty stores throughout New England. However, most maple producers are part time and have other jobs to provide more steady income and benefits.

If you're thinking about getting into maple syrup production, you'll need to consider some important issues, namely: time and resources. When sap is ready to flow, you've got to be ready to harvest it. If you have a job that doesn't permit you to be flexible, it might be difficult for you to assure a successful harvest. You also need to think about resources, both in money and trees. Unless you've had some experience (maybe you come from a maple syrup farming family) and you're thoroughly prepared to leap full time into maple syrup production, it's probably best to start small, with another job to provide backup funds.

Pitfalls

It's difficult to make a living making maple syrup, unless you're prepared to make it a full-time endeavor and diversify your business to include other aspects of the sugaring industry. Most people are advised to look at maple syrup production as a supplemental income, perhaps combined with another type of agricultural venture, such as dairy farming.

Perks

People have been making maple syrup for centuries, and not without good reason. There is consistent demand for maple syrup, and with proper marketing, you probably won't have any trouble selling what you produce. Making maple syrup allows you time outside, and puts you in touch with other producers, who tend to be a tight-knit, friendly group of people.

Get a Jump on the Job

If there's a maple producers association in your state, contact someone about joining it. Visit some farms that produce maple syrup and volunteer to help. Some farms may accept interns, so visit your state association's Web site and look up as many individual farms as possible.

MUSHROOM GROWER

OVERVIEW

You've probably seen those little knobs of fungus growing on fallen tree logs, under leaves, and popping up out of your lawn after a spring rain. But these wild mushrooms are just country cousins to the kind of mushrooms commercially grown in vast mushroom houses in northeastern Pennsylvania.

Commercial mushroom cultivation started in the Kennett Square area in the 1800s, for no real climatic or agricultural reason—it's just where the immigrants decided to plunk down a mushroom bed. It also helped that the environs of Philadelphia were near the major metropolitan areas of New York and Washington, D.C. As the industry grew, other support activities settled in the area, and the industry—well, it mushroomed.

By 2004, 857 million pounds of mushrooms were grown in the United States, more than half of which were produced in Pennsylvania, which represents the largest cash vegetable crop in the state. Sadly, although the growth of mushrooms is booming, the days of the small mom-and-pop mushroom farm are over. Just as in other types of agriculture, smaller farms find it economically difficult to compete. In the early 1970s, there were more than 300 mushroom farms in Kennett Square; today, there are 85.

If you've got a yen to nurture mushrooms, there are lots of different jobs you could consider in the industry. You can get

AT A GLANCE

Salary Range

Varies greatly depending on whether you own your own mushroom farm, and how large a farm you have, but hard workers with their own sizeable farm can make $50,000 or more.

Education/Experience

No specific degrees are required to be a mushroom grower, but it helps to have knowledge of topics relating to mycology. A degree in mycology or biology is helpful, depending on what aspect of mushroom growing you're interested in. For small mushroom farmers, classes or seminars on running a business (especially marketing skills) also would be useful.

Personal Attributes

You should have a good amount of determination, and be willing to work hard and put in long hours during the harvesting season.

Requirements

You must be physically able and reasonably fit to withstand hard work.

Outlook

The outlook for small mushroom farms is not especially good, since more and more farms are being consolidated into bigger operations. However, mushroom sales in general are extremely strong and growing.

a degree in mycology (the study of mushrooms) and do lots of different things, including research and development. Or you could decide to work in the marketing end of the mushroom business, trying to get more and more people interested in eating and buying mushrooms.

The actual process of growing mushrooms varies depending on the type of mushroom you're trying to grow. Basically you must provide a mushroom-growing medium, maintain correct temperatures, inoculate the medium with the spawn (seeds), and then harvest the mushrooms in separate harvests five to seven days apart. The "first flush" harvest is the best quality, because as the crop gets older, its quality and quantity decrease. (In between, there are incredibly complex tasks of sterilization, and constant monitoring of oxygen, ammonia, temperature, and moisture). From beginning to end, it takes between 11 and 13 weeks to harvest mushrooms.

Pitfalls

Growing mushrooms takes long hours on a daily basis; at times, conditions aren't

---

Jim Angelucci, general manager at mushroom farm

You could say that mushrooms are in his blood, growing up as he did in the midst of the country's mushroom capital—Kennett Square, Pennsylvania. Jim Angelucci's dad—as well as the parents of most of his friends—all worked in the business, and so it's no surprise that he's also been involved in mushroom growing all his life. For the past 32 years, he's been working in just about every capacity for Phillips Mushroom Farms in Kennett Square—a company that first started growing the fungi back in 1927. He started out as an assistant grower, but says that "just about everything there is to do on a mushroom farm I've done."

After a stint in the navy, Angelucci started his own small mushroom farm, but eventually discovered the cost of doing business was too high. It wasn't helped by the 1970 botulism scare that sent mushroom prices through the floor. Angelucci left the farm for economic reasons, and signed on to Phillips, where's he's been happily working with fungus ever since.

"Mushroom growing is a very labor-intense industry," he notes, "and still most of the harvesting is done by hand. This is a 24/7 business. Although some newer operations have a way to mechanize moving the equipment around, the rest of us are still doing it the way we did 100 years ago."

Phillips stopped growing the ubiquitous white button mushrooms some years ago. Today, they concentrate on portobello and crimini growing in the typical beds, plus shiitake, maitake, king oyster, and pom-pom mushrooms on sawdust logs. They also grow oyster mushrooms on cottonseed hulls and wheatstraw, and enoki and beach mushrooms in sterilized substrate in bottles.

"Growing mushrooms is like any other agricultural endeavor," Angelucci says. "It isn't as much a career as a lifestyle. Unless you're willing to spend long hours, it's not something you would want to do."

Still, it's a growing business. The industry has made major leaps in the last few years. "Up until the last six years, we didn't have anyone on the staff trained in mushrooms, but today we have a fungal geneticist. The industry is looking to the future.

"It's a fascinating career to be able to produce food for human consumption," he says. "And it's very rewarding. It's more difficult to grow mushrooms than it is to grow orchids."

really good. If it's Christmas morning, the mushrooms don't know that—they still have to be harvested.

Perks
Mushrooms are a finicky but fascinating fungus, and growers say they really enjoy working in the business because of the uncertainty and the fascination with this complex type of plant.

Get a Jump on the Job
These days it's not so easy for young people to get a job growing mushrooms, although it's possible to land a seasonal job doing some type of work on a large farm. If you're really interested in growing mushrooms, try landing any sort of job on a mushroom farm and then keep your eyes and ears open, watching how mushrooms are grown, harvested, and packed.

ORCHARD OPERATOR

OVERVIEW

If you're thinking about a career as an orchard operator, you're joining an American tradition that extends back almost 400 years. Apple trees and most other common fruit trees are not indigenous to America, but once they got here, they flourished. Grown for centuries in Europe and other parts of the world, the first American apple orchard was planted in 1625 in Massachusetts by a clergyman named William Blaxton. Blaxton's farm was in the Beacon Hill district of Boston.

Apple orchards quickly became very important to colonial people, who relied heavily on apples as a dietary staple. Because apples keep well after they're harvested, many households used them as a primary source of sustenance during the winter months.

As other seeds and seedlings were brought into the colonies, orchards became more widespread and common. John Chapman, more commonly known as Johnny Appleseed, was instrumental in popularizing apple growing throughout the Midwest, encouraging settlers to establish homesteads at the sites on which his trees were planted.

Today, there are thousands of orchards throughout the United States, ranging in size from a few trees to many acres; the average size of an American orchard is 50 acres. Some orchards contain only one fruit, while others produce a variety of fruit throughout the year, but in either case, the trend is to allow customers to pick their

AT A GLANCE

Salary Range

Salaries for those working in fruit production vary greatly, depending on the size of the operation, the location, how and where the fruit is marketed, and other factors. The average earnings of a full-time orchard operator working for a large orchard facility ranges from $32,620 to $81,100. Many orchard owners, especially those with small operations, rely on outside income to supplement their orchard income.

Education/Experience

A degree in agriculture or a related area is highly recommended. Agricultural jobs are becoming increasingly complex and require business skills as well as agricultural knowledge. Some colleges and universities offer majors such as farm business management and finance, which combine agricultural courses with courses in areas such as marketing, human resource management, finance, and strategic thinking.

Personal Attributes

An orchard operator must be willing to work long hours, especially at certain times of the year. Orchard work can be hard and dirty, and may require substantial physical endurance. You should be a problem solver, as situations can arise quickly that require sound decision making. Also, you should be able to get along with, and to manage people, as you'll be dependent on workers to harvest your crop and help with other tasks.

Requirements

Some knowledge of equipment and equipment repair; an understanding of growth patterns, irrigation and other related topics; and general knowledge concerning weather.

Outlook

Overall, the outlook for employment in all agricultural jobs is expected to decline by about 15

(continues)

own fruit. Some orchards have on-premise stores to sell fruit raised there, and sometimes other merchandise as well.

If you want to make orchard work your career, you'll be working year-round, although most of your efforts will take place in the summer and fall. Winter months are spent pruning the trees, which must be completed while the trees are dormant. In addition, trees must be kept well fertilized, and weeds among the trees must be cut down. In the spring, some of the immature fruit must be removed from the trees in order to produce a better quality crop in the fall. Once a fruit crop has taken hold and is on its way to being ready for harvest, you need to watch carefully for disease—par-

Richard Frecon, orchard operator

Richard Frecon remembers the good old days, when people weren't so particular about how their apples looked. Those were the days of the great big apple trees, when pickers would climb toward the sky on ladders to pick off the top branches.

Frecon, who has worked in his family's Boyertown, Pennsylvania, orchards for more than 50 years—nearly his entire life—says everything changed in the orchard business when consumers decided they liked their apples to be a solid red color, not mottled green and red.

"I guess it was back in the '50s or so when everybody got to like solid red apples," Frecon recalls. "When the apples were on those great big trees, the ones on the insides of the trees didn't get red because the sun couldn't reach them way back there. It wasn't easy to sell those apples, so we went to dwarf trees."

Dwarf trees have worked out well, and there's no going back. In fact, he says, there's no room for looking backwards when you're a fruit grower. It's extremely important to keep up with the latest methods and trends, always working to be more efficient and turn out a better crop.

The 185-acre orchard has been in Frecon's family since his father bought it in 1943. In addition to apples, he grows peaches and nectarines, all of which are sold locally from the on-site farm stand and to area supermarkets. The fruit also is sold to brokers for resale, and some of it is shipped overseas, primarily to South America.

Frecon depends on seasonal help to harvest his crop, using computers to keep track of payroll records, planting and harvest statistics, and other information. He urges anyone interested in operating an orchard to study agriculture, agribusiness, or a related field, and to be willing to work hard and keep thinking ahead.

Orchard work is not easy or particularly lucrative, Frecon says, but it gets into your blood until you can't imagine doing anything else. "I've done this for a long time and I don't know what I'd do instead," he says. "But it all depends on what you want. If you want to be on the fast track and make a lot of money and enjoy all the finer things in life, this probably isn't the business for you. But if it gets in your blood and you're willing to give up some of those finer things, it might be the best job you ever could have."

ticularly mold during rainy seasons—and insect infestations. Most orchard operators rely on pesticides to control pest problems, but a growing trend is toward integrated pest management, which is a more natural way of keeping pesky critters at bay.

These days, the trend in fruit production is to grow fruit on dwarf trees. While smaller trees have some advantages over the bigger trees of yesteryear, they also pose some challenges to growers. The main advantages of growing fruit on dwarf trees are that harvesting is much easier and the crop is more uniform. Gone are the days of fruit pickers perched precariously on high ladders, balancing the large bags they'd wear in which to deposit the picked fruit! And because the sun reaches all the fruit at about the same rate on smaller trees, they fruit ripens evenly and has a more uniform appearance. On the other hand, dwarf trees also have some disadvantages. Although the fruit is much easier to pick, the fruit is also easier for deer to nibble. Dwarf trees also require much more water than bigger trees because their roots are shallower.

If you're going to be a fruit grower, it's very important to understand not only how fruit grows, but the desirable properties of the fruit you're growing. Customers are increasingly choosy these days, demanding fruit that is uniform in color, of particular sizes, and blemish free. Understanding the various markets for different fruits is very important, as people of different cultures and geographical locations value different types of fruit.

Operating an orchard demands not only agricultural know-how, but also good business skills. Marketing, handling financial and tax considerations, organizing personnel, and arranging for fruit to be packed and shipped are just some of the tasks you'll need to be prepared to do.

Orchard work can be difficult and frustrating, due to circumstances beyond your control. There's nothing worse, fruit farmers say, than watching helplessly as hail batters and destroys the tender blossoms that might have been your apple crop.

Still, if you're meant to grow fruit—to watch those blossoms turn into tiny apples that grow and ripen all summer, then to harvest and send them on their way—operating an orchard might be the perfect career for you.

Pitfalls

As with any aspect of agricultural work, growing fruit can be unpredictable due to weather, insects, disease, and other circumstances that are beyond your control. And you may need to depend on seasonal help, which sometimes results in staffing difficulties because workers aren't always committed to their work.

Perks

If you love being outdoors and working in nature, you'll have a good time operating an orchard. Growing fruit can provide immense satisfaction, and you get to work independently. Your problem-solving skills will sharpen as you're called upon to resolve challenges of many kinds.

Get a Jump on the Job

If there's an orchard near your home, head on over there and ask if there's any work for you. It's a pretty safe bet that there will be. Try to stay on at an orchard for an entire year to experience the full growing season and seasonal work. Also, read everything you can about growing fruit and operating an orchard.

ORGANIC FARM MANAGER

OVERVIEW

It may seem simple enough: Farmers jump on a tractor, plow up some fields, plant seeds, and watch stuff grow. Farm managers watch other people do the work. While that may sound straightforward and simple, it can be anything but that! Until you've spent time on a farm, you may have little idea of the complexities involved with its operation—and an organic farm can be even more complex.

"Organic" farming means that no pesticides are used in producing the food or animals. In the old days, people took the farmer's word for it, but these days the best organic farmers are certified organic—which can entail quite a bit of paperwork. Most states have their own organic certification programs that meet the standards of the U.S. Department of Agriculture's National Organic Program.

Specifically, organic meat, poultry, eggs, and dairy products come from animals that are given no antibiotics or growth hormones. Organic food is produced without using most conventional pesticides; fertilizers made with synthetic ingredients or sewage sludge; bioengineering; or ionizing radiation. Before a product can be labeled "organic," a government-approved certifier inspects the farm where the food is grown to make sure the farmer is following all the rules necessary to meet USDA organic standards. Companies that handle or process organic food before it

AT A GLANCE

Salary Range

The national mid-range salary for a full-time, salaried farm manager is around $44,000, with the highest paid earning more than $81,000 and the lowest paid earning less than $24,500.

Education/Experience

Farming in general is getting increasingly complex, and running an organic farm necessitates particular knowledge and skills in addition to the general business and farming demands of a non-organic operation. For those reasons, a bachelor's degree in business with a concentration in agriculture is likely to be required in order to manage an organic farm.

Personal Attributes

You should like spending time outdoors and have a keen interest in and appreciation of the ways of nature and the properties of organic farming. Most people who farm organically do so because they're committed to raising foods without chemicals and being good stewards of the land—not just because they want to farm. You also will need to be organized, have good business skills, and be able to work effectively with people. Managing a farm, after all, isn't just about planting and harvesting.

Requirements

In addition to educational requirements, some practical farm experience is likely to be necessary. Many people in farming grew up on family farms and participated in youth agricultural programs, such as 4-H youth educational programs. Those who didn't grow up on farms may need to work on farms in different positions before they're able to qualify as a farm manager.

Outlook

In the past years, smaller farms have been consolidated into large operations, with many family-owned farms going out of business. Other smaller

AT A GLANCE

farms, however, have found niches that enabled them to grow and prosper. Organic farming is one of those niches, particularly in areas with populations that appreciate and demand organic foods in restaurants and grocery stores. Organic farming, in fact, although still limited, is the fastest-growing sector of agriculture. Awareness of organic farming is increasing, and many consumers are getting more and more interested in the benefits of eating foods that have been grown without chemicals.

gets to your local supermarket or restaurant must be certified, too.

Along with the national organic standards, USDA developed strict labeling rules to help consumers know the exact organic content of the food they buy. The USDA Organic seal proves that a product is at least 95 percent organic. And the government means business: People who sell or label a product "organic" when they know it does not meet USDA standards can be fined up to $10,000 for each violation.

"Natural" and "organic" are not interchangeable. You can use truthful claims such as free-range, hormone-free, and natural, on food labels, but only food labeled "organic" has been certified as meeting USDA organic standards.

As farm manager, you'll be expected to manage all the organic business aspects of the farm operation, including hiring workers, monitoring prices of seeds and supplies, ordering supplies, negotiating with banks or other lenders to get good financing deals when necessary, and keeping track of the organic certification paper-

work. You also may be responsible for marketing the farm and its products and finding customers.

To make things even more complicated, some organic farms participate in community supported agriculture (CSA), in which the farm sells shares of its anticipated crop to community members before the crop is even planted. This not only guarantees buyers for the coming crop, it reduces the farm's risk as far as fluctuating crop prices and changing markets because the consumer has already paid for the food.

In addition, a farm manager often is responsible for assessing production, keeping records of materials and supplies that are used, tracking buyers, and keeping up with governmental regulations that may affect farmers. You'll also need to keep up with farming trends, both here and in other countries, environmental laws and local regulations, and requirements regarding organic farming.

Managing an organic farm is challenging, but there is the potential for it to be a rewarding and personally satisfying career. This is not a field, however, that you can enter without education and training. All state university systems within the United States have one land-grant university that includes a school of agriculture. And, once you're working as a farm manager, you can pursue certification as an accredited farm manager, offered through the American Society of Farm Managers and Rural Appraisers.

Pitfalls

Managing an organic farm requires a high level of expertise on various levels, so

Amy Sprague, organic farm manager

Amy Sprague is on maternity leave at present, but until their daughter was born in 2004, she was the full-time manager of the organic Wolf Pine Farm she owns with her husband, Tom Harms, in Alfred, Maine. The farm provides organic food for more than 200 families in southern Maine and New Hampshire through a community supported agriculture program, in which families buy "shares" of the farm, entitling them to fresh, seasonal fruits, herbs, and vegetables. There also is a farm store where customers can purchase locally raised and produced meat, cheese, and eggs from other area farms.

Amy, who grew up in Maine, has always enjoyed the outdoors, but never considered farming as a living until she was in college at Boston University, where she studied environmental policy and analysis.

"It sort of came to me in college," she says. "I did a study abroad program in my sophomore year that sort of got me thinking about farming." Once she started thinking about farming, she found it difficult to stop.

After graduating from college, she worked as an environmental educator and farm apprentice for the Massachusetts Audubon Society, and managed a children's garden as part of a job as a teacher/naturalist at an environmental education center. In the summer of 2000, she worked as an apprentice at Drumlin Farm in Lincoln, Massachusetts, finishing shortly before she and her husband Tom bought Wolf Pine Farm.

Those work experiences, she says, were extremely valuable because she learned about many aspects of farming and managing a farm, including how to set up greenhouses, how to coordinate planting and harvesting, planning crops and overseeing the day-to-day operations. She encourages anyone interested in being a farm manager to look for internships and complete at least one, but preferably two or more.

Farming and managing a farm is hard work, Amy says, and requires many skills. You should be attentive to details, interested in business, willing to talk to people about what you do, and willing to roll with the punches.

"You're always battling weather and conditions, and things break down that you've got to fix," she says. "If you let all that get to you, it can really weigh you down. You've got to be able to go with the flow and be flexible, because nothing ever goes the way you planned."

Despite the challenges, Amy and her husband find great satisfaction in owning and running an organic farm. They love to be outside, and the community supported agriculture program means that in season, there are always people on the farm, giving Amy a chance to talk to them about the advantages of organic farming, land preservation, and other topics that are important to her.

"You really have to be passionate about what you're doing, and you've got to do it because you love it," she says. "You don't go into farming to climb the ladder and move into a better job. You do it because you find reward in it and because it's what you want to do."

preparing for the job can be a bit cumbersome. And, while many organic farms have been very successful, farming is always a risky business, due to varying factors such as demand, price fluctuations, and unpredictable weather.

Perks

If you thrive on the demands of a job that presents different challenges and opportunities daily, you may very much enjoy managing an organic farm. And people associated with organic farms tend to be committed to both farming and preservation of the environment, meaning it's a good bet that you'll work with thoughtful, socially responsible coworkers.

Get a Jump on the Job

If you're still in school, join a 4-H or other agricultural program if there's one available and you're not already a member. If there's an organic farm in your area, or even a non-organic farm, apply for a job during the summer or after school. Express your career interests and tell the farmer you're interested in learning how a farm operates. Read books and articles about organic farming in order to better understand what sets it apart from standard farming methods and its principles. Some organic farmers hire interns who are interested in learning about farming and farm management.

OYSTER SHUCKER

OVERVIEW

Americans have had a love affair with oysters stretching back at least to the mid-1700s, when diners enjoyed the tasty bivalves in a very rough cellar saloon in New York City, and where, presumably, the first oyster shuckers plied their trade. By the 1800s, oysters were firmly entrenched in the American restaurant scene, and shuckers were busy opening up oysters in oyster houses, stalls, bars, and lunchrooms in coastal cities. Once railroads were established and the shellfish could be transported, even people in cities further inland could enjoy oysters.

There's still huge demand for fresh oysters in the United States, particularly those from the Gulf of Mexico. The oyster industry in the Gulf states—Alabama, Florida, Louisiana, Mississippi, and Texas—provides a large profit, although the hurricanes of 2005 affected production.

The job of an oyster shucker is fairly straightforward. A shucker extracts oysters from their shells in order to prepare them to be eaten raw, cooked, frozen, or packed. Technique for shucking oysters varies widely, but usually either you hold the oyster firmly in your non-dominant hand or against a block, and force a shucking knife between the halves of the shell at its hinge. You then twist the knife in order to sever the strong muscle that holds the shell closed, and pry open the shell to expose the oyster. The oyster is then cut from the shell and flipped into a container.

AT A GLANCE

Salary Range

The average hourly rate for an oyster shucker is about $9.10 an hour, but an accomplished shucker working in a fancy restaurant or oyster bar can earn twice that much, plus tips.

Education/Experience

No formal education is required to shuck oysters. Traditionally, in fact, many of the best oyster shuckers learned their trade early and never received much formal education. Today, however, if you're looking to shuck oysters in restaurants, you may need to have completed high school and had some additional culinary training, or perhaps completed a two-year associate's degree in an area relating to culinary arts.

Personal Attributes

You must be able to stand for long periods of time, and be able to concentrate on what you're doing, despite distractions. If you're shucking in a restaurant, you'll be expected to be friendly and able to chat with customers.

Requirements

You must have the strength and ability to open oysters quickly while not destroying the look of the oyster by cutting it. It requires a fair amount of practice to be able to shuck oysters efficiently, and, if you're working in a restaurant where people can watch you, you need to make it look effortless. It takes lots of experience to become an accomplished oyster shucker.

Outlook

As mechanisms and techniques are developed and refined for extracting oysters from their shells without human labor, the demand for commercial oyster shuckers working in processing plants will continue to decline. However, some areas (such as New Orleans) have reported shortages of accomplished restaurant oyster shuckers, despite the offer of relatively high wages.

If the oyster is to be eaten raw, it's usually cut from both sides of the shell but left lying on the shallow half of the shell for serving. A good oyster shucker knows how to use a sharp knife to find a weak spot on the oyster's shell. Twisting the knife at the weak spot makes it easier—and faster—to get the oyster opened.

Megan Mack-Nicholson, oyster shucker

Megan Mack-Nicholson has been an official oyster shucker for only about a year and a half. If she dares to say so, however, she's not half bad. "There are some people who are faster than I am, but there are some who are a lot slower, too," she says. "When somebody asks me for a dozen shucked oysters, I try to get them to them within five minutes at the most. But that's not just shucking the oysters. That's getting them plated, as well."

Plating oysters at Maxie's Supper Club and Oyster Bar in Ithaca, New York, is no small feat, seeing that each order is accompanied by cocktail sauce; horseradish that's freshly grated by the server directly onto the plate just before serving; fresh lemon; and minuette sauce (similar to a vinaigrette dressing).

"If you can shuck and serve a dozen oysters in less than five minutes, you're doing pretty good," she says.

Mack-Nicholson learned about oysters and how to shuck them after several months on the job at Maxie's as a service assistant. In addition to shucking oysters, she also works as a bartender. On nights when it's not too busy, she's expected to shuck and mix drinks. When the oyster bar gets too busy, she moves to one post or the other. For the most part, she says, shucking oysters is a pretty good job.

"I find it fun, and you get a little workout while you do it," she says. "It's fun because people are watching you while you do it."

There is one aspect to shucking oysters, however, that Mack-Nicholson really does not enjoy. "It's no fun when you get a bad oyster, I'll tell you that," she says. "When you get one, you know it, that's for sure!"

Another downside to shucking oysters is the probability that sooner or later you'll end up with a pretty nasty cut. "I wear plastic gloves because I'm handling food, but I don't use the chain gloves that stop the knife from cutting you," she says. "For one thing, I'm left-handed and the glove doesn't fit me that well, and I just don't really like wearing gloves when I work." Actually, Mack-Nicholson says, you have a better chance of cutting yourself on the shell of the oyster than on the knife.

"Almost everyone here who shucks oysters has had a cut bad enough to send them to the hospital," she says. "I probably should have gone to the hospital once, but I took care of it here."

The secret to successful shucking is to learn how to quickly locate the hinge of the shell, and how to get your knife in to pop the hinge open. "The trick is to get your knife in between the lip so you can pop the hinge," she says. Once you learn how to do that, it's only the repetition and the danger of cutting yourself that gets wearing. Serving oysters, either on a plate or in a vodka drink called an oyster shooter, is the easy part.

If you're planning to be an oyster shucker, Mack-Nicholson suggests you make sure you're in fairly good physical condition, and find someone who knows what they're doing to work with you while you're learning. After that, it just takes practice.

Shuckers work either in processing plants or in restaurants. The best oyster shuckers in restaurants can open up to 250 oysters an hour—or about four oysters a minute. Experienced shuckers in processing plants shuck about 26 gallons a day.

In the past, shuckers in processing plants were paid for every gallon of oysters they separated from their shells. In 1924, the going rate for shucking a gallon of oysters was 25 cents, which rose to 35 cents by 1942, when many shuckers began leaving the processing plants to get better-paying jobs in the military. Because oyster harvesting is a seasonal business, during peak harvesting seasons shuckers may be required to work long hours, standing along processing tables opening oysters by the hour.

It's a bit of an easier life in the restaurant business, where restaurant shuckers normally work in an open area of the restaurant so that customers can watch them shuck their oysters. These shuckers are expected to know about different varieties of the shellfish, of which there are many. Oysters fall into six main categories, but they also vary within those categories depending on where they are raised or harvested. You also need to know about different kinds of oysters, because the shells of some varieties are softer or harder than others, so you need to treat them a bit differently when opening them.

Pitfalls

Shucking oysters isn't an easy job, and sooner or later you'll end up with a pretty nasty cut—especially if you don't wear protective gloves. Moreover, to make good wages you've got to find a job in an upscale restaurant where the spectacle of all those oyster shells splitting open makes the shucker more of an entertaining attraction than an employee. Restaurant work entails long, irregular hours, including nights (often late nights) and weekends. If you live in a rural area that's not located near a coast, there may be a shortage of restaurants that serve oysters and require the services of an oyster shucker.

Perks

As long as people keep eating oysters, there will be a demand for oyster shuckers. So, if you can learn to shuck oysters and become accomplished at the craft, you probably won't have much trouble finding work—as long as you live in an area where there are restaurants that serve oysters.

Get a Jump on the Job

If there's a restaurant near you that hires an oyster shucker, ask the restaurant manager and the shucker if you can watch the shucker work. Try to get to know the shucker, so you can ask questions about techniques and tools. Once you have an idea of how oyster shucking is done, you can buy a knife and some oysters and start practicing. But be sure to wear gloves! Even experienced oyster shuckers wear gloves, to protect them from the sharp oyster knives that have to be able to cut through the muscle that attaches the oyster to its shell.

If you're interested in the restaurant business in general, enroll in a culinary arts program or school, or look for a community college or other college in your area that offers culinary training.

PARK RANGER

OVERVIEW

If your idea of heaven is to walk through the outdoors on a quiet summer morning, listening to the chirps of the birds in the trees and watching the sun come up over the mountains in the distance, you might enjoy working as a park ranger in the National Park Service. With more than 76 million acres of national parks under its jurisdiction, the U.S. National Park Service and the park rangers it hires have the job of educating and ensuring the safety of the millions of visitors who hike, climb, ski, boat, fish, and explore these natural resources.

Park rangers manage historical, cultural, and natural resources such as wildlife, forests, parks, lakeshores, seashores, historic buildings, battlefields, archaeological properties, and recreation areas. They also help to conserve resources in national parks and other federally managed areas, helping with forest or structural fire control.

The primary responsibility of the park ranger is safety. Rangers must strictly enforce outdoor safety codes and ensure the compliance of campers, hikers, and picnickers, enforcing laws and regulations, investigating violations, complaints, trespassers, and accidents, and helping to perform search and rescue.

But there are also lots of other jobs to be done: Education is another important aspect of their job, and park rangers are often called upon to provide natural, historical, or scientific information to park

AT A GLANCE

Salary Range

The starting salary for rangers hired in the summer (with a college degree) is $18,687; permanent ranger positions begin at $20,908 to $31,680, depending on college degrees and experience; top salary after 10 to 15 years of experience is about $37,000.

Education/Experience

Rangers need at least a bachelor's degree, with a major in natural resource management, natural or earth sciences, history, archeology, anthropology, park and recreation management, law enforcement/police science, social or behavioral sciences, museum sciences, business or public administration, sociology, or other closely related subjects. Rangers should have administrative, professional, technical, or investigative experience that provided a familiarity with natural or cultural history, fish, or wildlife habitat characteristics, techniques of resource protection and use, recreational use of public lands and facilities, enforcement of laws, rules, or regulations, or fire prevention and suppression.

In lieu of a college education, candidates must have at least three years of experience in parks and conservation and must demonstrate an overall understanding of park work. A working knowledge of law enforcement, management, and communication skills also enhances your prospects.

The orientation and training a ranger receives on the job is sometimes supplemented with formal training courses. Training for duties that are unique to the National Park Service is available at the Horace M. Albright Training Center at Grand Canyon National Park, Arizona, and the Stephen T. Mather Training Center at Harpers Ferry, West Virginia. In addition, the Park Service makes use of the training center in Brunswick, Georgia.

Personal Attributes

Good communication skills, flexibility, interest in working with the public, love of nature and outdoors.

(continues)

visitors. They also develop interpretive material for the natural, historical, or cultural features of an era, and in some positions may demonstrate folk art and crafts. They also operate campgrounds, including such tasks as assigning sites, replenishing firewood, and leading guided tours. Differences in the exact nature of duties depend on the grade of position, the site's size, and specific needs.

You can find a park ranger in the city, the suburbs, or out in the countryside, but more than half of all park rangers work in areas east of the Mississippi River. Although you'll usually find them outdoors, there are times rangers must work in offices, especially as they are given more managerial responsibilities. If you think you'd like to be a ranger, you should be comfortable with moving around, because most rangers can expect to be assigned to several different parts of the country during their careers. There's no guarantee that you'd be stationed in only one area.

Depending upon your qualifications, you'd begin service at different levels (called

grades), moving up through the ranks to become district ranger, park manager, or staff specialist in interpretation, resource management, park planning, and related areas. At upper levels, rangers' responsibilities and independence increase as their influence covers more staff and area.

Upper-level managers in the Park Service are recruited primarily for their managerial capabilities, but there is competition for park ranger positions at all grades.

Pitfalls

Landing that first job as a park ranger is one of the toughest parts of this job, which can be almost impossible what with the low turnover and lack of new openings. Many rangers begin in low-level entry positions, working summers or part time, emptying trash or maintaining trails. Some rangers find that the inability to choose where they'll spend the rest of their working life is also a drawback. In addition, the income tends to be fairly low.

Perks

The fact that these jobs are so hard to come by is evidence of the desirability of this job—what could be better than going to work each day in a national park, surrounded by woods, clean air, and abundant wildlife? If you love the outdoors, there's probably no better job than a park ranger that combines stewardship of the land with the sheer enjoyment of being out in nature.

Get a Jump on the Job

You might start out trying for part-time or seasonal work at national, local, or

Mike Connolly, interpretive park ranger

As a young boy Mike Connolly fell in love with the outdoors, and he managed to turn his fascination with nature into a full-time job, working with the U.S. Forest Service and the National Park Service since 1997 as an interpretive park ranger. "I just loved working outside," he says. "I love learning about the natural resource I'm involved with, and educating people about the outdoors." As a high school student, he contacted a local park and asked them what he could do to help out on weekends. By the time he went to college, he knew that national parks were his destiny, and he majored in natural resources planning and interpretation at Humboldt State University. "That's a very specific degree, but very few schools in the country offer that degree on a bachelor's level. Most rangers study more of a broad-based field."

Interpretive park rangers serve as a liaison between the natural resources that they administer and the public, helping to explain wildlife, natural resources and cultural resources, geology, botany, and astronomy. In the spring, Connolly works as an interpretive volunteer park ranger at Lava Beds National Monument in northern California, home to the Modoc Nation. Connolly spends his summers as an interpretive park ranger at King's Canyon. That's because getting a permanent job in the National Park Service is very challenging, and there are very few positions available.

"When you apply to a well-known national park such as the Grand Canyon, it's not uncommon for them to hire 10 seasonal employees—but it's not unusual to have 300 or 400 people applying for one job. Not as many people have heard of Lava Beds—they probably have 50 or 60 competitors for one job. Most people start as either student conservation associate or as a volunteer working anywhere from 16 to 32 hours a week," he says. "From there, they can earn experience and eventually become a seasonal employee."

During a typical day when he's at King's Canyon, Connolly might open up the visitor center and make sure everything's ready to go. Since his primary task is interpretive programming, he might offer a guided walk or an evening program. "Conducting those requires a ton of research and preparation," he says, "making sure not only that the gear is functional but that there's been enough advertising to let people know about the program. There's also a lot of preprogramming, and then interacting with public. At the end of the day, you wrap up, close the visitor center, and keep track of the statistics for Congress and the Park Service and get ready for the next day."

In the meantime, Connolly has his name in for two permanent positions in California. "Personally, I know at least 100 other people I'm competing with," he says. If he doesn't get either job, it's back to King's Canyon for his seasonal hitch from May through September. "I've been living the seasonal life for seven years," he says. "You have to be able to move all the time. If you're willing and able to move a lot, that's important. I haven't heard of any park rangers who have stayed at one park. Most have worked at multiple parks. I still have flexibility, but I don't like the fact that I can't call one place home."

Despite the low pay and the uncertain job future, Connolly still loves his work. "After all, I get paid to be outside enlightening the public, teaching the public how special the natural resources of this country are. When I work with children and get them to ooh and ahh over something this national park has to offer, that's the most rewarding thing going."

state parks if you're interested in someday becoming a park ranger. You also could contact your local park to see if you could volunteer on weekends, or do a special internship project. With current tight budgets, there is always something that needs to be done. Every single person in the United States lives within a day's drive of a national park, so if you're interested in this career, reach out and see what volunteer opportunities you might come up with.

PEANUT FARMER

OVERVIEW

You eat them on sandwiches and pour them on top of your banana split, but did you know that there are at least 298 other uses for peanuts, including as an ingredient in paper, inks, and oils? Chemist George Washington Carver came up with all of them, but declined a patent on peanut butter because he considered food products to be gifts from God.

When it comes to actually growing peanuts, President Jimmy Carter is probably the most famous peanut farmer in the country, but in fact there are hundreds of others of his ilk out there in the southern United States.

Peanuts aren't really nuts at all, but the seed of an annual legume, which grows close to the ground and produces its fruit below the soil surface—and typically grows no farther north than Virginia, since a climate with 200 frost-free days is required for a good crop. Warm weather conditions, adequate moisture, and fertile, sandy soil result in the appearance of peanut leaves in 10 to 14 days after planting.

The peanut is grown in tropical and subtropical regions throughout the world, but it's native to the western hemisphere. Historians suspect the peanut originated in South America and spread north and east with Spanish explorers. By the 1700s and 1800s, a few colonists in America were growing peanuts, but because this was thought of as food for the poor, and since growing and harvesting techniques were

AT A GLANCE

Salary Range

Difficult to predict, depending on area of the country and size of farm, but may range from $14,325 to more than $30,000.

Education/Experience

No formal training or credentials, but knowledge of peanut farming is essential to success and an agricultural education offered by land-grant universities in many states is beneficial. Typical coursework covers the agricultural sciences and business subjects such as accounting and marketing. Whether it is gained through experience or formal education, peanut farmers need enough technical knowledge of peanuts, growing conditions, and plant diseases to make sound scientific and business decisions.

Personal Attributes

Experience in peanut farming helpful; farming also requires business skills, so it's helpful to have taken courses in business or a bachelor's degree in business with a concentration in agriculture or farm management.

Requirements

It's crucial for peanut farmers to stay abreast of the latest developments in agricultural production, new cost-cutting procedures, new forms of marketing, or improved production using new techniques. County cooperative extension agencies serve as a link between university and government research programs and farmers, providing the latest information.

Outlook

As with all types of farming, consolidation of farms and increasing prices makes this a challenging occupation. Peanut farmers face touch decisions as prices don't increase much while mortgages, credit, and cost of machinery and labor rise.

Wes Shannon, peanut farmer

Wes Shannon has been farming for most of his life, and he's been farming his 500-acre spread for the past 27 years. "I was raised in farming," he says, "and I never had any doubts about what I wanted to do when I was growing up. Although maybe," he chuckles, "I've had some doubts sometimes since!" Shannon, a member of the advisory board of the Georgia Peanut Commission, is also Georgia's representative on the National Peanut Board.

Most of Shannon's peanuts are sold to major shellers, and most of his peanuts probably end up in peanut butter. In fact, he says, most of the peanuts in Georgia are used for peanut butter, salted nuts, or candy.

On a typical spring day, Shannon starts his planting day at 7 a.m., loading peanut seed in 50-pound bags into planter hoppers. He plants 120 pounds of seed an acre, so he's constantly lifting bags up into the hopper and driving the tractor up and down rows, for 10 to 12 hours. After the peanuts are planted, he spends the summer cultivating, watching the plants grow, and dealing with pests. Harvest begins after Labor Day, with the inverter plowing up the peanuts, lifting them, and turning them upside down. After about five to seven days in the sunshine, the combine comes through, separating pods from vines.

Part of the fun of harvesting is nibbling the ripe peanuts right off the vine. "Although by the end of the harvest, you get tired of eating them," Shannon says. The family also roasts some of the peanuts for themselves, or fries them like French fries. Another peanut delicacy on the farm is to eat green peanuts, before they're ripe. "You take some green peanuts and boil them in a pot in their shells, just like peas," Shannon says. "Then you open the soft shell and eat them like fresh peas or beans." Boiled green peanuts, however, is an acquired taste that isn't particularly popular in other parts of the country.

Shannon's farm in Tipton is in south-central Georgia. He says he's lucky to have grown up in peanut farming, because starting out brand new in today's Georgia would be almost impossible. "Purchasing land is almost out of the question, although you could rent land from some retired farmer. The profit margin is pretty slim and the hours are long, especially if you're just starting out. And the cost of equipment is almost prohibitive. There are much easier and better ways to make a living!"

Of course, that doesn't mean he doesn't love what he does. "The trade-off for the big bucks is knowing that you're growing a wholesome product people can eat and use for food, a product that's helping to keep our country self-sustaining. Instead of peanuts coming from somewhere else, we're eating our own products. Just planting the crop and watching it grow, watching how the Lord blesses us with the rain, it's hard to describe. If you've never watched a plant grow, it would be hard to understand it."

There are other benefits of being a peanut farmer that Shannon thinks are hard to measure. "Raising children on a farm seems to give them more of a sense of values in life," he says. "They get a better appreciation of things around them. My son is 15 now, but by age 5 he'd seen animals being born and animals dying. Had he not been on the farm he'd never [have] had that opportunity."

not easy, there were not very many peanut farmers until after the Civil War. By the end of the nineteenth century, new equipment and processing techniques boosted the nascent peanut industry, and by the twentieth century—with George Washington Carver's research—the demand skyrocketed for peanut oil, roasted and salted peanuts, peanut butter, and peanut candies. It was Carver who suggested that farmers could plant peanuts as a rotation crop in the cotton-growing areas of the south, which is still done to this day. Today, most peanuts are grown in just seven states: Georgia grows the most peanuts, followed by Texas, Alabama, North Carolina, Florida, Virginia, and Oklahoma.

Seeds are planted in rows and rotated every three years with cotton, small grains, or corn, to avoid disease. In the fall, harvest begins with a digger that loosens and lifts the plant from the soil, turning the plant upside down, so that the pods can dry in the sun. After drying in the field for a few days, the combine removes the pods and leaves the vines on the ground to improve the soil. Freshly harvested pods are then cured to reduce the moisture content for safe storage. After curing, the farmers' peanuts are graded to determine the overall value by the Agricultural Marketing Service of the U.S. Department of Agriculture at buying stations or shelling plants usually located within a few miles of the farm. Once the grade is established, the loan or commercial value is determined from USDA price support schedules.

Pitfalls

During the planting, growing, and harvesting seasons, peanut farmers are busy for long hours, often longer than an eight-hour day and a five-day, 40-hour week; work cannot be delayed when peanuts must be planted and harvested. Living conditions are often modest, with low wages and lack of benefits, and farmers risk exposure to pesticides and other potentially hazardous chemicals.

Perks

If you enjoy being outdoors and working on your own, and have a special interest in peanuts and watching plants grow, you could be very happy as a peanut farmer.

Get a Jump on the Job

There's usually lots of extra work to do on a peanut farm, so if you're an enterprising sort and you'd like to learn more about raising peanuts for a living, consider trying to get a summer or after-school job on a peanut farm.

RANGE MANAGER

OVERVIEW

Most of us know about the range from watching movies featuring a cowboy loping along on his horse across the range—miles and miles of rolling grasslands unbroken by trees. Vast rangelands still exist in the western United States, carefully watched over by range managers trained to protect plants for forage, wildlife for aesthetics and hunting, and clean water.

Rangelands are a classification of unforested land that isn't part of developed agriculture. Although a lot of rangelands are used as pasture—grazing is one of the major uses of rangeland—they aren't the same as introduced pastures, where the farmer has planted and fertilized certain grasses ideal for grazing. Instead, rangelands are managed in their native state.

Range managers work for federal and state agencies, colleges and universities, private industry, environmental groups, and on foreign assignments. Some range managers work for federal or state agencies, planning and directing public and private land use. Others are researchers, teachers, and extension agents with colleges and universities. Private industries hire range managers as ranch or land managers, agricultural product sales and service representatives, land reclamation specialists, and environmental consultants.

Range managers, also called range conservationists, range ecologists, or range scientists, study, manage, improve,

AT A GLANCE

Salary Range

Median annual earnings of conservation scientists in 2002 were $50,340. The middle 50 percent earned between $39,300 and $61,440. The lowest 10 percent earned less than $30,630, and the highest 10 percent earned more than $70,770.

In 2003 most bachelor's degree graduates working for the federal government as range managers started at $23,442 or $29,037, depending on academic achievement. Those with a master's degree could start at $35,519 or $42,976. Holders of doctorates could start at $51,508. Beginning salaries were slightly higher in selected areas where the prevailing local pay level was higher. In 2003 the average federal salary for rangeland managers was $53,657.

Education/Experience

A bachelor's degree in range management or range science is the usual minimum educational requirement for range managers; graduate degrees usually are required for teaching and research positions. More than 30 colleges and universities offer degrees in range management. A number of other schools offer degree programs in range science or in a closely related discipline with a range management or range science option. Specialized range management courses combine plant, animal, and soil sciences with principles of ecology and resource management. Desirable electives include economics, statistics, forestry, hydrology, agronomy, wildlife, animal husbandry, computer science, and recreation. Selection of a minor in range management, such as wildlife ecology, watershed management, animal science, or agricultural economics, can often enhance qualifications for certain types of employment.

Personal Attributes

Good communication skills, interest in wildlife and the outdoors, patience.

AT A GLANCE

Requirements

The Society for Range Management offers certification as a professional rangeland manager (CPRM). Candidates seeking certification must have at least a bachelor's degree in range science or a closely related field, have a minimum of five years of full-time work experience, and pass a comprehensive written exam.

Outlook

Slower-than-average job growth is projected because of limited growth in government; most employment opportunities will be in private sector consulting. Demand will be spurred by a continuing emphasis on environmental protection, responsible land management, and water-related issues.

and protect rangelands to maximize their use without damaging the environment. Rangelands cover about 1 billion acres of the United States, mostly in western states and Alaska. They contain many natural resources, including grass and shrubs for animal grazing, wildlife habitats, water from vast watersheds, recreation facilities, and valuable mineral and energy resources. Range managers may inventory soils, plants, and animals, develop resource management plans, help to restore degraded ecosystems, or assist in managing a ranch. For example, they may help ranchers attain optimum livestock production by determining the number and kind of animals to graze, the grazing system to use, and the best season for grazing. At the same time, however, range managers maintain soil stability and vegetation for other uses such as wildlife habitats and outdoor recreation. They also plan and implement revegetation of disturbed sites.

Working conditions vary considerably. Although some of the work is solitary, they also deal regularly with landowners, farmers, ranchers, government officials, special interest groups, and the public in general. Some conservation scientists work regular hours in offices or labs. Others may split their time between fieldwork and office work, while independent consultants and especially new, less experienced workers spend the majority of their time outdoors overseeing or participating in hands-on work.

Most range managers work in the U.S. Department of the Interior's Bureau of Land Management, the Natural Resource Conservation Service, or the Forest Service. Another 20 percent of conservation scientists and foresters work for state governments, and about 10 percent work for local governments. The remainder work in private industry, mainly in support activities for agriculture and forestry or in wood product manufacturing. Some are self-employed as consultants for private landowners, or federal and state governments. Range managers work almost entirely in the western states, where most of the rangeland is located.

Pitfalls

The work can be physically demanding. Some range managers work outdoors in all types of weather, sometimes in isolated areas, often called to prevent erosion after a forest fire, and they provide emergency help after floods, mudslides, and tropical storms. And the controversies and lawsuits involving rangeland management can be unpleasant for some individuals.

Perks

If you enjoy working outdoors, you'll have a wide variety of opportunities.

Get a Jump on the Job

In high school, take courses in biology, chemistry, speech, English, math, and zoology. Experience in agriculture (4-H and FFA) is desirable.

Doug Powell, Bureau of Land Management rangeland manager

Protecting wildlife was Doug Powell's dream when he was in college at the University of Nebraska. "When I went to school, they offered a degree in natural resources, and I started out in wildlife protection. But because there were a lot of job opportunities in range management, I decided to emphasize both to improve my chances of getting a job."

As Powell explains it, rangeland managers primarily manage vegetation in order to try to maintain native conditions, the productivity of land, and to reduce erosion. "They tend to be a little bit of a generalist, and they may have some involvement with wildlife programs because of their efforts in maintaining habitat for wildlife." In addition, Powell says, they may be involved in recreation, because recreation issues could have an effect on the productivity of rangeland. For example, off-highway vehicles could cause erosion problems that could affect soil and rangeland conditions.

In general, Powell explains, rangeland managers are associated with grazing programs because a lot of rangelands are used for grazing by domestic animals. "We rangeland managers are quite concerned with how lands are grazed and how that affects plants," he says.

In his position as rangelands manager, he tries to make sure that research scientists publish on rangeland issues is made available to other range specialists within the Bureau of Land Management. "My job is to coordinate between the agency and professional societies," he explains.

Quite often, rangeland managers are hired by the federal government for agencies such as the Forest Service or the Bureau of Land Management, the Natural Resources Conservation Service, or the Fish and Wildlife Service. Rangeland managers typically would be heavily involved in grazing programs, responsible for administering grazing permits that allow individuals to use public lands. They also may be involved in wildlife habitat, reclamation efforts, and so on.

"As a rangeland manager," he says, "I might look at managing a piece of rangeland that I've identified, checking out the desired plant community, at wildlife habitat, at the native wildlife that use the area." A lot of the job of monitoring rangeland conditions is documenting productivity and the makeup of plant communities and how that might change under whatever present management is.

"So, I've got a certain amount of grazing, and, in monitoring the area, I detect that the plant community was changing in unhealthy ways. I might suggest that grazing practices be changed. A lot of rangeland management has to do with measuring plant populations to see if you're getting more desirable plants."

TIMBER HARVESTER

OVERVIEW

Timber is harvested in every state, but more people are employed in this field in the West and Southeast, where there are an abundance of private and national parks and forests. About half of all timber harvesters work for the government, usually at the state or local level.

Harvesting timber entails several jobs. If you're a faller, your job will be to cut down trees with high-power chain saws. You'll probably be required to wear a hard hat, eye and ear protection, boots, and safety clothing. A bucker trims the tops and branches off the fallen trees and cuts the logs into specified lengths. Choke setters fasten cables or chains around the logs so they can be dragged out by tractors or moved onto self-propelled forwarders that move the logs.

Other workers sort, mark, and move logs, inspect them for defects, measure them, and estimate their value. These workers normally record data into handheld devices that later can transfer the information via modem to a central computer.

There also are equipment operators, who use tree fellers to cut trees and grapple loaders to lift and load logs into trucks. Logging equipment is getting increasingly high-tech, with some of it equipped with computer equipment that requires skilled operators with considerable training. Unless you have prior training or experience, you're likely to begin in the timber harvesting business with responsibilities that require manual labor. As you gain

AT A GLANCE

Salary Range

Up to $30 an hour, depending on the employer and the type of harvesting. Owning and operating your own logging business can net yearly earnings of $30,000 to $40,000 to start, and up to $80,000 once your business is established.

Education/Experience

Little formal education is required for most timber harvesting jobs. Some vocational-technical schools and community colleges, however, offer courses or a two-year degree in forest harvesting, general forestry, or conservation. Having completed courses or earned a degree may be helpful in getting a job, or getting a job with a higher salary.

Personal Attributes

You'll need to have physical strength and endurance, along with good judgment, because harvesting timber requires the ability to make quick decisions about potential hazards. You must be able to work as part of a team and be willing to work outdoors every day.

Requirements

You'll probably need a driver's license in order to get to job sites, unless you stay on site or your employer provides transportation. Depending on your particular job within a logging operation, you may need to know how to operate machinery used in the harvest of timber. Some states require harvesters to be certified through a university extension program, and more states are pushing for required certification.

Outlook

Overall employment of timber harvesters is expected to decline slightly between now and 2012. This is due to several factors, including increased mechanization and increasing imports from countries who can sell timber for less because workers are paid less to harvest it. However, the potential opening of forest lands to timber harvest may offset the projected decline in jobs in this field.

experience, you'll be trained to operate expensive equipment and machinery.

The job of a timber harvester is not easy. In fact, it is considered to be more hazardous than most jobs, due to falling trees and branches and the use of sawing machinery. Weather conditions can cause hazards to increase, and sometimes force timber harvest to halt. Wind can create dangerous conditions for timber harvesters, and mud can cause the ground to become slippery and hazardous to workers using power equipment. Hearing loss also can occur over time if precautions are not taken.

Logging training programs vary depending on your employer, but you should receive some type of classroom and/or field training in several areas, including safety, business management, endangered species, reforestation, and management practices. You probably will get special training if you're going to be harvesting trees that are exceptionally large or which have wood that is valuable. It's important to learn how to cause the least amount of

Randy Walters, timber harvester

Randy Walters grew up in a logging family and followed in the footsteps of his father, who began harvesting timber in 1942.

Most of Walters' jobs come to him through logging consultants, who serve as liaisons between people who have lumber to sell and those who cut and process it. The average length of a job he takes is between three and four weeks, during which time he and a small crew will cut timber with a total volume of 80,000 feet.

Before Walters agrees to take on a harvesting job, he needs to understand the expectations of the property owner and/or the logging consultant representing the property owner. If he believes that he can meet those expectations, or the owner is willing to be flexible, Walters reviews and signs a contract, agreeing to certain terms regarding the work to be done, a time frame, price, and so forth.

He receives a down payment, hires a crew of loggers to work with him, and begins the job. "All jobs vary from one to the next," Walters says. "Nothing ever happens the same way." For that reason, timber harvesters need to be flexible.

Some jobs may require loggers to build roads to transport logs and equipment, and staging areas where logs can be initially processed. Equipment used in logging includes a tractor and trailer; a skidder, which is used to pull trees from the woods; chain saws for hand felling; and log loaders and mechanical cutters for cutting smaller trees.

Generally, Walters and his crew will proceed to a logging site, at which trees to be cut have been marked or the cutting area is otherwise designated. Depending on the type and size of the trees, they'll be cut either with chain saws or with mechanical cutters, trimmed, pulled from the woods and loaded into the trailer of a truck.

Walters owns a facility in Brandamore, Pennsylvania, where he further processes lumber and sells it. He leaves the wood he cuts in pieces as large as possible, allowing customers more options in how the wood may be used.

He says he has about 10 primary customers for his wood, including companies that manufacture veneer, door frames, and molding; furniture makers; and lumber mills. Basically,

damage possible to the tree you're cutting and the trees surrounding it.

Depending on for whom you're working and where you live, you may have a long commute between your home and the site on which you'll be harvesting timber. That can make for long workdays, sometimes leaving home before dark and returning back home after dark.

Some loggers start and operate their own businesses, which gives you more flexibility and opportunity. However, it takes substantial capital to purchase the necessary equipment, and it's necessary to have business skills in order to successfully start and run a logging operation.

Pitfalls

The work is hard with many hazards: falling trees and limbs, the required use of saws and other power equipment, bad weather, poisonous plants, biting insects, and snakes and other pests of the woods. Harvesting timber is physically and mentally demanding, as you must be aware

Walters says, he knows which customers want which types of wood, making the job of selling it fairly easy. Much of his best-quality woods, such as poplar, gets shipped to woodworkers in Italy.

While Walters enjoys his work, it is by no means an easy way to earn a living. The days are long, the work is hard and the pay is not top notch.

It's not unusual for him to get up very early to take wood to a sawmill, return to a logging site to harvest timber all day, and then tend to paperwork at night.

"Sometimes I get up at twenty after three in the morning to drive to a sawmill and then I'll come back and I'll work all day," Walters says. "Then, when I get home that night, there's paperwork that needs to be done."

And Walters, who is 52, finds the physical work of harvesting timber more demanding than he used to.

Regulations regarding timber harvest are increasing, and Walters strongly recommends education and training for anyone thinking of getting into the field. It's especially important to know about sustainable forestry and forestry management, he says, which calls for logging techniques that do not significantly damage forests.

"I know some people who basically want to sell their lumber, cash in, and get what they can," he says. "But that's generally not the best way to go. If you don't do it right today, where are you going to go to cut timber tomorrow?"

If you want to be a timber harvester, he suggests you be prepared to work long hours, especially if you have your own business. You also should be physically equipped to do hard, physical work.

"It's not an easy business, that's for sure," Walters says. "You've got to want to do it and be willing to work hard. If you go home at five o'clock every night, you're not going to be in business very long."

and alert to hazards to yourself and the members of your work team at all times.

Perks

There is chance for advancement in timber harvesting for those who work hard and are diligent about learning. Many harvesters tend to be outdoors people who are much more inclined to cut trees in the woods than sit inside at a desk.

Get a Jump on the Job

If you know how to drive a truck or bulldozer or can operate a crane, you may have a head start in the business of harvesting timber, since operating that type of machinery is necessary to the job. Check to see if your vocational-technical school has a forestry or related program, or if such a program is offered through a university extension service in your area. You also can get ahead by learning all you can about different types of trees, the value of their wood, and where and how they grow.

TOPIARY GARDENER

OVERVIEW

If you've ever been to zoos, parks, or stately homes, you've probably seen them looming over the crowds: great green leafy creations in astonishingly lifelike poses—elephants, camels, horses, or geometric shapes. These fanciful living sculptures are called topiary, and the people who create them are called topiary gardeners. Topiary gardening—the art of fashioning living plants into ornamental shapes—has been practiced for centuries; the Egyptians and Romans were the first to use topiary and prune plants into decorative shapes. They chiseled boxwood into sailing ships and trained cypress trees to create hunting scenes. The resulting forms were given the Latin name *topiarii* (landscape gardener, from *topiarius*), a word related to such complicated outdoor work.

Plenty of plants make good topiaries. Topiary gardeners may work with English ivy trained on wire globes, dark-green perennial Wilson ivy, and the *euonymus Coloratus*, with reddish-purple foliage in winter. They may clip African mallow, with dazzling pink flowers throughout the growing season that can be trimmed in spring to train into standard topiary. Or they may choose a tropical firecracker vine, twining with tiny red-trumpet blooms around a wire obelisk.

If you're interested in being a topiary gardener, there are generally two directions to choose: You can work for one of the very large national horticultural display gardens, such as Longwood Gardens

in Pennsylvania or Cypress Gardens in Florida, or for beautifully decorated theme parks with world-famous topiary, such as Walt Disney World and Disneyland. (New highlights at Walt Disney World in 2004 included a Magical Gathering topiary garden featuring Mickey Mouse, Minnie Mouse, Goofy, Pluto, and Donald Duck.) Alternatively, you can go into business for yourself as a private consultant, or branch out and set up your own topiary business.

Whichever career path you choose, the basics of topiary remain the same. You'll start with artists' models and drawings, creating blueprints and full-size steel frames to guide the growth of the plant you'll use to match the design.

Shrubs that shear well, are naturally full, and are fairly fast growing produce the best shrub topiary. The first step in the production of a shrub topiary is to fill the container with a well-drained soil mix and that provides support for even the largest figures. Shrubs are planted at each place where the frame comes into contact with the soil.

For example, a reindeer with four feet on the ground will have a plant in the center of each of the four legs, the longest and most appropriately shaped one becoming the neck and head. On the other hand, if your frame is a ballerina dancing on one toe, your job gets much harder, since the entire structure must come from a single plant.

After the shrubs are positioned and planted, the frame is placed over them

Renee Worrell, topiary gardener

The next time you're vacationing at the Walt Disney World Resort and you look up in awe at the plant-filled topiary camels, dancing elephants, trained seals, giraffes, Mickey and Minnie Mouse and Donald Duck, think of Renee Worrell, who's been working in the nursery at the popular Florida theme park for the past 25 years. "I feel quite blessed to be able to work where I do," she says. "And I'm lucky to work with a lot of people who inspire me."

Topiary gardening, the art of fashioning living plants into ornamental shapes, has been practiced for centuries. Found throughout the gardens of the Walt Disney World Resort are hundreds of topiary figures, ranging from traditional hedges and sheared trees to fanciful shapes and a whole menagerie of "chlorophyll" Disney characters.

Worrell started out in the landscape field and took horticulture classes—at a time when there weren't a lot of women in the field. During the construction of Epcot Park, she got into topiaries. At the time, the park was using topiaries filled with woody shrubs, which can take from three to 15 years to finish, depending on size. Because Disney was growing, there was a need to produce topiaries faster. So they moved on to sphagnum moss-filled topiaries, which, once the form is ready, can be placed in the park within a month. "Our first one was an elephant," she says. "Then we ventured into a large birthday cake for the Magic Kingdom Park. It was quite a learning experience, because there's a lot of internal structure, and it made the topiary really heavy." Sphagnum topiary frames must be heavy-duty since they are the only support for these figures.

Sphagnum topiary produce quick results. After heavy steel frames are stuffed with sphagnum moss, small plants such as creeping fig and English ivy are planted in the moss. Wax begonias or impatiens may be used to add color. After the plants are inserted in the moss figure, it is almost ready to go. "There are so many different plants we haven't tried yet!" Worrell says.

"We challenge ourselves to get the characters correct," she says. "Mickey has to be a certain size, in proportion to his body, so we work closely with the artists." This can be a challenge, because topiary are living plants that change from one week to the next, which can distort the character.

The nursery department is constantly checking over the more than 200 topiary frames they have in inventory. The topiary are used periodically for special events throughout the year. The largest group is produced for the Epcot International Flower & Garden Festival that is held each spring.

There are tricks to maintaining a topiary figure. "Irrigation is a real science," Worrell says. "In some big areas of topiaries, they stay wet, but others—like a finger sticking out—will dry in

and situated firmly in the soil, so that each plant stays at the proper level. The plants are then mulched with several inches of cypress mulch and watered.

It takes a lot of patience to be a topiary gardener. Producing a shrub topiary requires constant clipping, corrective pruning, tying, and weeding, as well as regular irrigation and fertilization. In order for the plant to fill in the entire frame, you must gently pull, tie, and prune it so it gets trained into the unusual pattern of growth needed to fill in ears, tails, antlers, wings, and so on.

Once the figure has matured, you must keep pruning a few inches from the frame

the wind." Each topiary has an internal irrigation system, with tubes going out to the fingers, to the top of Mickey's ears, and with irrigation heads that pop up and spray large areas. "We can isolate the belly and turn it on or off," Worrell explains, "but we have to watch it every single day." For example, sometimes squirrels like to burrow underneath the topiaries to pull out the moss, or the surrounding landscape must be sprayed, which will affect the topiary's plants.

"It's nice to be able to share knowledge, and network, really being open to different ideas. It's hard work doing topiaries but if you have creativity it's fun."

The frames take the longest time. If it's a Disney character, a Disney World Imagineer will create a wire sculpture and then cover it with clay, so they can move the arms and head around to get the desired affect. Once the character artists in Orlando and California approve it, it's cast into the figure called a maquette and then goes to a welder. The welder creates the frame that can take about a year from beginning to end.

"We work as a team," she says. "We encourage having people working together on projects. If we're trying something new, we can ask everyone's opinion." Worrell works in the Disney greenhouses about six miles from the Walt Disney World Theme Parks, next door to the Disney's Animal Kingdom Theme Park. The nursery supports hanging baskets, topiary, and specialty crops for all parks and resorts.

Worrell says students should have both field experience and education. "I took classes, and that really helped. Do some volunteer work in your community geared around horticulture and to see if that's for you," she says. The single most important thing a student could do is to check out AgrowKnowledge online (http://www.agrowknowledge.org), she says. AgrowKnowledge (the National Center for Agriscience and Technology Education) is a national partnership of community colleges with business, industry, associations, and schools that provide classes, job information, and much more.

"The horticulture field takes a lot out of you," she says, "but you get so much in return. It's very hard work, and you have to have a lot of enthusiasm. It's very rewarding." Even during busy times, when she's given a list of topiaries to get ready on short notice, or a shipment of plants arrived late, "it challenges you," Worrell says. "Then you're networking and getting back on schedule."

In the end, it's all worth it. "Disney is really a great place to work," she says. "There are so many people here who are so knowledgeable. It's a good place to grow!"

to keep them in shape, using shears, hand clippers, or electric grass shears. You must remove unnecessary branches to prevent woody stems and trunks from showing through the frame and to remove girdling branches and roots. It's important to known the plant material you're working with. For example, some materials will turn brown if you cut them with electric shears, while others won't turn brown at all. Shrub topiaries are clipped every week during the growing season and every two weeks during the remainder of the year.

Pitfalls

Jobs as a topiary gardener can be tough to find, and competition can be keen. There aren't that many large horticultural gardens or theme parks. If you're intent on earning a living this way, you may need to relocate to find work. If you can't find work at a large garden or park, you'll need to go into business for yourself, which requires initial start-up money and considerable business know-how.

Perks

If you love horticulture, art and design, and being in the outdoors, it's hard to find a better combination of all these interests than topiary gardening. Sculpting living things is the ultimate way to incorporate a love of nature and art, and the permanency of the design has an added value.

Get a Jump on the Job

If you're interested in topiary, your first step should be to find a topiary gardener and pick his or her brain about techniques and details. See if you can get a job on the weekend or summer as an assistant. You might try taking a local workshop in table-top topiary often offered at horticulture centers, home and garden centers, or public gardens. You also can get kits to start out with, forming topiary in shapes of animals. Try one and see what happens!

TURF SCIENTIST

OVERVIEW

You probably don't spend too much time studying what's under your feet as you walk across your lawn or sink a putt on the fourth hole. But studying the complexities of turf is big business for turf scientists, who combine good people skills with a scientific yen for horticulture.

If you choose to work as a turf scientist, you might work as a golf course superintendent, turf manager for a sports stadium, park or grounds manager for corporate headquarters, sod producer, lawn care professional, or sales representative for companies that produce turf care products. Or you could choose to go into research and teach at a land-grant agricultural university.

As a turf scientist, you'd probably start out caring for lawns, golf courses, park sites, athletic fields, or corporate grounds, using your scientific know-how to maintain turf, as well as to operate computer-controlled irrigation equipment and highly technical machines.

As turf scientists advance in their careers, they may become coordinators, managers, or assistant or branch managers in corporations. In these positions, they still must rely on their scientific expertise to make good purchasing decisions and to explain tasks to their employees, but much of their time is spent creating and managing budgets, coordinating projects, and managing an organization with numerous employees.

AT A GLANCE

Salary Range

$28,750 to more than $65,450.

Education/Experience

Minimum bachelor's degree with courses in turf management, soil fertility, weed science, plant pathology, entomology, and horticulture, along with courses in chemistry, algebra and calculus, accounting, management, business and technical writing, and communications.

Personal Attributes

Interest in science; good oral, written, and computer skills.

Requirements

None.

Outlook

Employment of turf scientists is expected to grow more slowly than average for all occupations through 2012. The need to replace turf scientists who retire or otherwise leave the occupation permanently will account for many more job openings than will projected growth.

Pitfalls

If you've studied turf science because you love nature and want to work outside, you might find the business end of this job to be a bit unexciting.

Perks

For individuals who love science, enjoy working outdoors, and have fun growing things, the job of turf scientist can combine all of these into one fun job. There's plenty of room for specialization and promotion.

Abby McNeal, Denver Broncos turfgrass manager

Abby McNeal knew she loved working in the outdoors in the landscaping field, but she wasn't exactly sure just where her path would take her. At Colorado State University, she explored a variety of courses. "I knew I didn't want an office job," she says. "My college program had several concentrations, and turfgrass was one of them. After one semester, I liked it." Fascinated by the world of plants and landscaping, she graduated with a B.S. in landscape horticulture with an emphasis in turfgrass management.

From there, she landed her first job with the city of Westminster, Colorado, where she was hired to oversee a grow-in of a brand new 28-acre soccer park. "They were finishing the subsurface," she recalls, "and getting ready to seed it, when the contractor turned the project over to the city and I was hired for a seasonal position." After that, McNeal worked for the Boulder, Colorado, parks department at their state-of-the-art soccer complex. Then it was on to work as athletic turfgrass manager at the University of Colorado, and from there she moved to her job with the Broncos, where she is currently an assistant turfgrass manager at INVESCO Field at Mile High Stadium, helping in the development and implementation of the maintenance program and the painting regime.

"A lot of the things we do, we get instant gratification," she says, "painting or mowing the field. You can see exactly what you've done right and what you've done wrong. People are blown away, how quickly we can get the field back into shape. I guess I like the 'wow!' factor of the job."

She enjoys working for the Denver Broncos, who are well known for their superior field. They were the first in the United States to use a special stabilization system in the field called the GrassMaster, a natural grass field in which polypropylene fibers are planted amidst the roots of real grass. This can eliminate many of the problems with all natural grass, such as bare spots,

Get a Jump on the Job

To prepare for a career as a turf scientist, in high school try to take as much biology, chemistry, English, mathematics, and physics as possible. Other extremely helpful courses include public speaking, Spanish, and computer science.

mud pools, and divots. "It's Dutch technology," McNeal explains. "Basically, it eliminates the bare spots and you don't have to resod the middle of the field."

In addition to her work with the Broncos, she was chosen for three years for the turf crew for the Super Bowl. "Three years ago they asked some women turf managers if they wanted to do it, and I said yes. I've been asked back every year since then."

She admits it's still a tad unusual to find a woman managing turfgrass. She was the only woman in her college program, and the only student interested in sports turf at the time. "When I first got out of college, it was probably tougher to be accepted as a woman in this field than it is now," she says. "I'd like to think that I've taken positions and earned the ability to do the job as well as anybody else, so it doesn't matter what my gender is. It's still tough in some realms. I've been chewed out by coaches, just like the men have."

A two-time recipient of the Rocky Mountain Regional Turfgrass Association Professional of the Year Award, she's served as a board member of the Rocky Mountain Regional Turfgrass Association, the Rocky Mountain Turfgrass Research Foundation Board, and she was past president of the Colorado Sports Turf Managers Association.

She advises students to be willing to start at the bottom and work up. "My first internship was at a parks and recreation department. No matter what level you're at, be willing to do any job asked of you. I won't send an employee out to do any job that I wouldn't do." She suggests students might get a start working a summer job at a local parks and recreation department, or perhaps at a nearby university.

"You've got to like working in a variety of climates, under different stressful situations," she says. "If you like to work outdoors, this may be a good career."

WINEGROWER (VITICULTURIST)

OVERVIEW

You've probably seen pictures of vineyards in California, France, or Italy—miles of gently rolling hills covered with manicured rows of vines, laden with huge bunches of grapes. To a winegrower—the viticulturist—the planning, supervising, and growing of selected grape varieties to produce wine is a life's passion. (The winegrower is the viticulturist, working in the vineyards with the vines; the winemaker is called an enologist, and is concerned with what happens to the juice of the grapes once the grapes are harvested.) Together, the winegrower and the winemaker decide when and how the grapes should be harvested and the specific wine created. In smaller vineyards, the winegrower may also be the winemaker.

When it comes to wine produced in the United States, most people automatically think of California. But in fact, winegrowers can be found in all 50 states. Winegrowers can be found working for wineries, vineyard management companies, vineyard owners, processors of raisin and table grapes, and juice processors. No matter who the employer might be, the growing of grapes appeals to many types of people—from the outdoors person to the laboratory scientist, from the economist to the wine lover, from the ecologist to the engineer. No matter what sort of background the winegrower comes from, he or she is an expert in all things vineyard.

AT A GLANCE

Salary Range

Fluctuates wildly, depending on whether the grower is also the vineyard owner, works for a large or small vineyard, acts as consultant, and so on; winegrower consultants can earn $80 to $100 an hour.

Education/Experience

A basic agricultural and plant science education along with some type of bachelor's degree; degree in viticulture most helpful.

Personal Attributes

Interest and experience in horticulture and grape growing; able to analyze and solve problems; able to make accurate observations; good communication, interpersonal and organizational skills; flexibility and adaptability; and ability to work outdoors.

Requirements

None.

Outlook

Excellent. Interest in grape production has increased tremendously throughout the United States, which has created opportunities and challenges in new production areas. Opportunities are expanding for both hands-on winegrowers and for those in research and development as experts continue to improve vineyard management methods, harvesting techniques, environmental protection, water conservation, and the yield and quality of the grapes.

A winegrower typically determines all the important details about a vineyard, including which vines to plant, how to detect disease and analyze water, what kind of rootstock works best in different soils, when to prune, how to prevent mildew, how to kill the plant material under the vines, and much more. Winegrowers may find themselves pruning, trellising, and irrigating; fertilizing, testing for minerals, managing pests, or doing marketing and quality control. Scientific knowledge is increasingly important in viticulture, and some winegrowers specialize in the research and development of grape varieties. And because people are becoming more and more concerned about the environment and their health, winegrowers today often find themselves coping with a wide range of government regulations.

Peter Fanucchi, winegrower

To Peter Fanucchi, it's all about the flavors. There's nothing he likes better than to wander through his California vineyard, tasting the grapes he's nurtured since he was a boy, working side by side with his father. "I started learning with my father how to grow grapes," he recalls. "My father loved wine. His father was a farmer back in Tuscany." You could say that growing grapes is in Fanucchi's blood.

Today, his Fanucchi Vineyard produces between 350 and 650 cases of Zinfandel a year, and between 400 and 600 cases of Trousseau Gris. When his parents bought the small vineyard back in 1971, the land came with some very old vines, planted more than a century ago in the Russian River Valley in Sonoma County. "My father thought the vines were too old and decrepit, and he was planning on pulling them out," Fanucchi recalls. But when his dad died unexpectedly in 1981, Peter inherited the vineyard and decided to keep the old vines. It was an inspired decision, because those old vines can produce excellent wine. "There's more interest now in extreme flavors. We planted a new block of vines in 1981, but the other original block had been planted in 1901."

As Fanucchi worked in the 17 acres of his vineyard, he continued to learn from their neighbors, from textbooks at the university, and from the Sonoma county extension service. As the viticulturist, winemaker, and vineyard owner, Fanucchi does it all, everything from actually pruning grape vines to selling. As a small grower, he doesn't maintain his own winemaking facility; instead, he takes about a third of his grape crop to make his wine in another facility. The rest of his harvest he sells to other wineries. "I started my wine brand in '92," he says. "I've always been a farmer, growing the grapes, but only recently I've started making wine." As demand for his award-winning wine grows, he'll be able to use more of his own grapes for his own vintages, and will sell fewer grapes to other wineries. He's now sending his wines to the East Coast, in New York, Pennsylvania, New Jersey, Georgia, and Connecticut.

"One of the neat things about a small winery," he says, "especially one that grows red wines, is that in very different years you'll have very different wines. You can take eight years of my Zinfandel and put them side by side and they can be very, very different."

Developing and marketing wine takes up more of his time, but he's really happiest when he's walking through his vineyards. "I love to eat the grapes I've grown," he says. "As a kid I always loved to eat the ripe fruit off the vine. Wine grape flavors are more intense. You can make wine out of every grape, but the reason why we use the grapes we do is because of the great flavors they have."

(continues)

The life of a vineyard can vary dramatically depending on the type of grape. The Chardonnay, Pinot Noir, Merlot, and Cabernet Sauvignon grapevines last about 30 years if they don't contract a fatal disease. Other vines, such as the hardy Zinfandel, can live for more than a century.

(continued)

One of the reasons those grapes taste so good, he says, is that he never uses any herbicides or pesticides on the grapes. "I'm not registered organic because I don't like the paperwork, but I'm basically organic, because I don't use any pesticides or herbicides," he explains. "In wine grapes there isn't a whole lot of pesticide use, because we're not trying to make the grapes look good—we're just going to smash them. People are now interested in being as organic as they possibly can. Unlike when you grow fruits and vegetables that are a one-year crop, the quality of flavors in the grapes are due to the environment, where they're grown. The flavors are from that environment, so you want to keep it pure."

For example, Fanucchi works to organically prevent mildew, instead of treating it with chemicals after it occurs. "It's easier for me," he says. "If you've got hundreds of acres, a lot of guys use sprays to treat mildew. I can pretreat my little spot… it's a matter of me walking out there every day and seeing what's going on. Basically I walk through the vineyards when grapes start turning color. I have a habit of tasting the grapes long before they're ripe, before anyone else would. They're so puckery!"

Part of being a really good winegrower is being able to implement the right farming techniques on a moment's notice. "You have to be ready for whatever the weather does," he says. "It's a matter of being out there [at] the right time. Some of the bigger growers who have lots of acres, they don't have that flexibility." As the grapes begin to ripen, Fanucchi's job gets more complex. He's out in the vineyard every day, checking the grapes by taking samples and getting a chemical analysis. "But in our end of the business on a small scale, it's just as important to taste the flavor of the grapes. I decide when to pick when I've got the right flavors."

But harvesting is only part of the job. "You have to be a McGyver of sorts, using the tools you've got and fabricating stuff. My dad was an engineer. I know how to weld, I know how to draw things, I took some engineering courses." It seems as if there's always something to do around a vineyard. "I could prune all day," he laughs. "In the modern section of the vineyard, I call a company to prune. With the old vines—the Zinfandel—I've retrained over the last 20 years, so those I prune myself to keep those in balance. It's a combination of knowing the vineyard through experience and some scientific knowledge I've gotten from books and research and from seminars. If I hired someone to prune that vineyard they would either leave too many buds or too few and the quality would be mediocre to poor."

In spite of the vagaries of California weather and the constant hard work, it's clear Fanucchi loves his work. "People should do what they like to do. No matter what job you do, the most important thing is to like doing it. My passion is rooted in growing the best possible fruit that I can. My wine can age for a time, and then I can share the pride of what I did."

A winegrower also spends lots of time with the vineyard's winemaker, conducting various laboratory tests to monitor the progress of grapes to make sure of their quality and figure out the best time to harvest. The winegrower also organizes the crushing and pressing of grapes, the settling of juice, and the fermentation of grape material.

Harvesting is an important time in a vineyard, and the grower supervises, manages, and trains the workers who produce and harvest the grapes. The winegrower also must supervise the maintenance of the vineyard during the off-season. As a wine expert, the grower also may give guided tours, conduct tastings, and advise visitors about various aspects of wine or grapes. Record-keeping activities are another important part of the job.

Pitfalls

Working in a vineyard in some ways is much the same as any other type of agriculture—the work is never over. Certain jobs have to be done at certain times of the year during certain types of weather, no matter what. And growing grapes—and ultimately the success of a particular vintage year—is highly dependent on the weather, which can be unpredictable and destructive at times.

Perks

Working outdoors, enjoying nature, and nurturing the different varieties of grapes to try to concoct a truly great wine can be a wonderfully satisfying way to earn a living. Winegrowers tend to be passionate about their job and the pleasures of growing grapes.

Get a Jump on the Job

If you think wine growing sounds like a great job, you should plan to take courses during high school in the sciences, basic agriculture, and communications. Many county extension services (especially in New York and California) also offer courses and seminars in viticulture. Develop your own special interests as you go through school. You can then go on to study viticulture in one of the universities located in wine country, such as the most famous—the University of California/Davis, followed by Fresno State in California, and on the East Coast, Cornell. (Universities in other countries also offer majors in enology or viticulture, including the University of Stellenbosch in South Africa, the University of Adelaide in Australia, the University of Bordeaux and the University of Beaune in France, and the University of Guelph in Ontario, Canada.)

APPENDIX A: ASSOCIATIONS, ORGANIZATIONS, AND WEB SITES

AGRONOMIST

Agronomic Science Foundation (ASF)
677 South Segoe Road
Madison, WI 53711
(608) 273-8080
http://www.a-s-f.org

Foundation that provides leadership and financial resources to further the role of the agronomic, crop, and soil sciences in global crop production, and to promote human welfare within a sustainable environment.

American Society of Agronomy (ASA)
Crop Science Society of America
Soil Science Society of America
677 South Segoe Road
Madison, WI 53711-1086
(608) 273-8080
http://www.agronomy.org

The ASA is a prominent international educational society that shares a close working relationship with the Crop Science Society of America (CSSA) and the Soil Science Society of America (SSSA), also sharing the same headquarters office staff. Each of the three societies is autonomous, has its own bylaws, and is governed by its own board of directors. Society members are dedicated to the conservation and wise use of natural resources to produce food, feed, and fiber crops while maintaining and improving the environment. ASA is a scientific society meeting the needs of its members through publications,

recognition and awards, placement service, certification programs, meetings, and student activities. Its science policy office in Washington, D.C. gives members a voice in government.

ALPACA FARMER

Alpaca Owners
& Breeders Association, Inc.
17000 Commerce Parkway, Suite C
Mount Laurel, NJ 08054
(800) 213-9522
aoba@ahint.com
http://www.alpacainfo.com

The Alpaca Owners & Breeders Association supports alpaca farmers by providing information about getting started in farming, breeding alpacas, selling fleece, locations of other alpaca farmers, and so forth. Formed in 1988, just four years after alpacas were first imported into the United States, it sponsors conferences several times a year and publishes a magazine (see below). Its Web site contains links to other alpaca-related sites, both domestic and foreign.

Alpacas Magazine
Alpaca Owners and Breeders
Association, Inc.
(856) 439-1076

Published five times a year by the Alpaca Owners and Breeders Association, Inc., Alpacas Magazine *provides the latest news on alpaca-related topics. Articles* inform readers about the latest alpaca research, provide marketing tips, and list upcoming conferences, alpaca shows, and human interest stories.

BEEKEEPER

American Honey Producers Association (AHPA)
http://www.americanhoneyproducers.org

The American Honey Producers Association (AHPA) was formed to promote the common interest and welfare of honey producers. The group has an extensive membership and lobbies on a national level for the interests of beekeepers and honey producers. It also holds an annual convention.

American Beekeeping Federation, Inc.
PO Box 1038
Jesup, GA 31545
(912) 427-8447
http://www.abfnet.org

The American Beekeeping Federation was founded more than 50 years ago to serve the needs of beekeepers. It serves as a legislative liaison, a clearinghouse for information, and an advocate for beekeepers. It also holds an annual convention and publishes a bi-monthly newsletter and annual member directory.

Bee Culture magazine
The A.I. Root Company
623 West Liberty Street
Medina, OH 44256
(216) 725-6677
http://www.beeculture.com

A monthly magazine for beekeepers, Bee Culture keeps subscribers up to date about the science and business

of keeping bees, the latest industry innovations, legislative issues of interest and locations of other beekeepers.

Go Beekeeping.com
http://www.gobeekeeping.com

A comprehensive Web site, including the history of beekeeping, links to other organizations, information about free classes in beekeeping, and much more. The site was created and is maintained by Dana Stahlman, a master beekeeper who retired recently from his beekeeping business in Blacklick, Ohio.

BUFFALO HERDER

The Buffalo Guys
Box 74
Elk Mountain, WY 82324
(888) 330-8686
http://www.thebuffaloguys.com

The Buffalo Guys is a company that raises buffalo and sells their meat by mail order, in health food and gourmet stores, and to restaurants. The Web site, however, also includes useful information about the history of buffalo, raising buffalo, and buffalo meat. Also, the site contains news concerning buffalo and the buffalo industry, and links to other buffalo-related sites.

Neal Smith National Wildlife Refuge and Prairie Learning Center
PO Box 399
9981 Pacific Street
Prairie City, IA 50228-0399
(515) 994-3400
http://www.tallgrass.org

The refuge is open to the public, who can view buffalo and their calves, elk, badgers, deer, native grasses and flowers, and more. There also is a state of the art nature center and many educational opportunities. For those who can't visit the wildlife refuge, the Web site contains a comprehensive overview and a wealth of educational material.

Dakota Territory Buffalo Association
PO Box 4104
Rapid City, SD 57709
(605) 923-6383
http://www.dakotabuffalo.com

Formed in 1996 by a group of buffalo producers from 12 states and two Canadian provinces, the association works to educate the public about the buffalo industry and to raise awareness about buffalo and buffalo meat. Organization members are dedicated to preserving buffalo as wild animals. The organization hosts an annual winter conference and a yearly buffalo show and sale.

National Bison Association
1400 West 122nd Avenue, Suite 106
Westminster, CO 80234
(303) 292-2833
http://www.bisoncentral.com

The National Bison Association was founded in 1995 when the National Buffalo Association and the American Bison Association merged. The organization, which strives to create a profitable, sustainable market for buffalo meat producers, has about 1,500 members in all 50 states and 16 foreign countries. It also works to educate the public about matters regarding the American bison.

BUG WRANGLER

Bugs Are My Business (Steven Kutcher)
http://home.earthlink.net/~skutcher

This fascinating Web site includes all sorts of information about insect wrangler Steven Kutcher, including lists of articles about him, books he's published, film credits, and his lectures and notes on entomology and open spaces.

CHRISTMAS TREE GROWER

National Christmas Tree Association
16020 Swingley Road, Suite 300
Chesterfield, MO 63017
(636) 449-5070
info@realchristmastrees.org
http://www.realchristmastrees.org

The National Christmas Tree Association works closely with many state and regional associations to help represent them and promote the use of real trees. The organization has more than 5,100 members. The Web site contains valuable educational information.

***Christmas Trees* magazine**
PO Box 107
Lecompton, KS 66050
(785) 887-6324
http://www.christmastreesmagazine.com

Published quarterly, Christmas Trees magazine provides information for Christmas tree growers on various aspects of production, including planting, marketing, shearing, shaping, and weed control. Published by Tree Publishers, Inc., Lecompton, Kansas, the magazine has been used by wholesale and retail tree growers for 31 years. It is an independent publication, not associated with any company, organization or association.

CITRUS GROWER

UltimateCitrus.com
http://www.ultimatecitrus.com
This Web site contains links to all the major Florida citrus producers, citrus packers, the Florida State Department of Agriculture, the Florida Horticultural Society, the Florida Citrus Production Research Advisory Council, the Florida Agricultural Statistics Services, citrus labelers, and many other groups. It also contains general information about weather in citrus-producing regions and the history of citrus production in Florida and other citrus areas. There are links to other informative sites, as well as on online shop.

AgricultureLaw.com Fruit Links
http://www.agriculturelaw.com
Links are provided on this Web site to more than 50 organizations related to fruit production, including citrus. The linked sites contain a variety of information about all aspects of fruit production, including growing, shipping, marketing, exporting, and regulatory concerns.

CRAB FISHERMAN

For general information on licensing crab fishing vessel captains, contact the U.S. Coast Guard Marine Inspection Office or Marine Safety Office in your state. Or contact any of the following agencies:

**Office of Compliance,
Commandant (G-MOC-3)**
2100 Second Street, SW
Washington, DC 20593
http://www.access.gpo.gov/nara/cfr/
waisidx_01/46cfr28_01.html

**National Maritime Center
Licensing and Evaluation Branch**
4200 Wilson Boulevard, Suite 630
Arlington, VA 22203-1804

Marine Technology Society
5565 Sterrett Place, Suite 108
Columbia, MD 21044
http://www.mtsociety.org

Potomac River Fisheries Commission
222 Taylor Street
PO Box 9
Colonial Beach, VA 22443
(800) 266-3904
prfc@crosslink.net
http://www.prfc.state.va.us

The Potomac River Fisheries Commission regulates the fisheries of the main stem of the tidal Potomac River from the Maryland/Washington, D.C. boundary line to the mouth of the river at Point Lookout, Maryland, and Smith Point, Virginia. The PRFC regulates all recreational and commercial fishing, crabbing, oystering, and clamming in the main stem tidal Potomac River, and issues licenses for those activities. The Potomac River Fisheries Commission coordinates regulations with the Maryland Department of Natural Resources, the Virginia Marine Resources Commission, and the Department of

Game and Inland Fisheries, and with the other Atlantic coastal states through the Atlantic States Marine Fisheries Commission.

CRANBERRY FARMER

Cape Cod Cranberry Growers' Association
http://www.cranberries.org

The Cape Cod Cranberry Growers' Association is one of the oldest farmers organizations in the country. Established in 1888 to standardize the measure by which cranberries are sold (the 100-lb. barrel), it has become one of the leading agricultural organizations in the state. The CCCGA has a professional staff that assists growers in solving everyday problems, offering assistance in regulatory compliance, sponsoring professional development seminars, and organizing association activities such as the Massachusetts Cranberry Harvest Festival every Columbus Day weekend.

Cranberries Magazine
PO Box 190
Rochester, MA 02770-0190
(508) 763-8080
http://www.cranberriesmagazine.com

The only publication devoted exclusively to growing cranberries, published since 1936.

The Cranberry Institute
3203-B Cranberry Highway
East Wareham, MA 02538
(800) 295-4132
http://www.cranberryinstitute.org/contactus.htm

A nonprofit organization founded in 1951 to further the success of United States and Canadian cranberry growers through health, agricultural, and environmental stewardship research as well as cranberry promotion and education.

Duxbury Bay Cranberries
PO Box 2268
Duxbury, MA 02331
(781) 834-8657
duxburybay@adelphia.net

Wisconsin State Cranberry Growers Association
PO Box 365
Wisconsin Rapids, WI 54495-0365
(715) 423-2070
http://www.wiscran.org/brochures.htm

Nonprofit organization that represents the interests of cranberry growers.

CROP DUSTER

National Agricultural Aviation Association
1005 E Street, SE
Washington, DC 20003-2847
(202) 546-5722
http://www.agaviation.org

With more than 1,300 members in 46 states, the National Agricultural Aviation Association is a source of information and support to the industry. The organization is affiliated with the National Agricultural Aviation Research and Education Foundation, which works to promote the safety and effectiveness of aerial agricultural spraying. The group also holds an annual convention. Its

Web site contains articles pertaining to the industry and a members-only site for those working as aerial agricultural applicators.

National Agricultural Aviation Museum
Mississippi Agriculture
and Forestry Museum
1150 Lakeland Drive
Jackson, MS 39216
(601) 713-3365
http://www.mdac.state.ms.us/Library/
BBC/AgMuseum/AgForMuseum.html

Agricultural aviation is just one of the attractions at this 37-acre museum complex, which also contains a model small town, complete with a school, church, jail, general store, blacksmith shop, and other attractions. The agricultural aviation museum features an actual old-fashioned crop duster plane.

DEER FARMER

Brand Deer Farm
http://www.branddeerfarm.bigstep.com

Deer farm owned by Dan Brand in Lewiston, Minnesota. Web site lists available stock and contact information.

Deer Farms Dot Com
http://www.deerfarms.com

This deer farm directory listing and advertising service offers lots of information about deer farming, venison recipes, bulletin boards, classifieds, information on getting started, and much, much more.

Maine Deer and Elk Farmers Association
info@mdefa.com
http://www.mdefa.com

Association for Maine deer farmers featuring photo contests, newsboards, and more.

North American Deer Farmers Association
1720 West Wisconsin Avenue
Appleton, WI 54914-3254
(920) 734-0934
http://www.nadefa.org

Association dedicated to the promotion of deer farming and ranching as an agricultural pursuit, which offers educational programs and publications. This is the largest deer farming organization in the United States and Canada, and provides advisory and referral services for those who are interested in the husbandry of cervidae.

Northeast Deer and Elk Farmers
http://www.ndef.org

Association of deer farmers of northern New England, originally The Northern New England Deer Farmer's Association. In 1998, the organization was renamed Northeast Deer and Elk Farmers to better reflect the change in the market area and the growing number of elk farmers. This organization offers a newsletter, helpful meetings, information, annual meetings, and special courses for members.

Quality Deer Management Association
PO Box 227
Watkinsville, GA 30677
(800) 209-DEER (3337)
http://www.qdma.com

A nonprofit wildlife conservation organization dedicated to ensuring a high-quality and sustainable future for white-tailed deer and white-tailed deer hunting. Founded in 1988, the QDMA currently has members in 48 states and several foreign countries, including more than 800 deer management professionals. The QDMA has developed numerous partnerships with state wildlife agencies, timber companies, hunting groups, and product manufacturers that have increased both the awareness of the QDMA and participation in the association's management philosophy— quality deer management.

DOWSER

American Society of Dowsers
PO Box 24
Danville, VT 05828
(800) 711-9530
http://www.dowsers.org

ASD has chapters and conferences throughout the United States dedicated to the teaching of dowsing as applied to varied disciplines

EMU FARMER

American Emu Association (AEA)
PO Box 224
Sixes, OR 97476
(541) 332-0675
http://www.aea-emu.org

A national organization that provides seminars, magazines, and an active Web site as they seek new ways to develop and expand this industry. The AEA encourages and promotes research, production, marketing, sales, and the commercial use of emu and emu products, encourages regulations supporting a viable emu industry, enhances the industry's public image,

and provides educational programs and publications as forums for subjects of special interest to the emu industry.

FISH FARMER

Aquaculture Magazine
http://www.aquaculturemag.com
Published by the World Aquaculture Society, the magazine contains not only news of the organization, but feature stories and general information about fish farming, as well. It also lists meetings, conferences, and other events related to the aquaculture industry. Published quarterly, the magazine is free to members of the World Aquaculture Society.

World Aquaculture Society (WAS)
341 Pleasant Hall
Baton Rouge, LA 70803
(504) 388-3137
http://www.was.org

Founded in 1970, the World Aquaculture Society is an international, nonprofit organization with more than 4,000 members in more than 90 countries. The organization was founded with the mission of bringing together the diverse global community of fish farmers. With international chapters in Japan, Latin America, the United States, and the Asian Pacific region, the organization works to improve communication and information exchange among aquaculturists from around the world.

FORESTRY CONSULTANT

USDA Forest Service
1400 Independence Avenue, SW

Washington, DC 20250
(202) 205-8333
http://www.fs.fed.us

The Forest Service, which manages America's 193 million acres of public lands, was founded in 1905 and is an agency of the United States Department of Agriculture. The Forest Service Web sites contains bountiful information about the organization and its work, as well as about public and private forestry, in general.

Evergreen magazine
PO Box 1290
Bigfork, MT 59911
(406) 837-0966
http://www.evergreenmagazine.com

First published in 1986, Evergreen magazine is the most widely read forestry magazine in the world. Published by the Evergreen Foundation, a non-profit organization that promotes forestry-related research and education, the magazine provides information about news and events that impact forests, foresters and those who use forests for recreational or study purposes.

GAME BIRD PRODUCER AND HUNT ORGANIZER

The North American Gamebird Association (NAGA)
1214 Brooks Avenue
Raleigh, NC 27607
(919) 515-5403
http://www.naga.org

Established in 1931, the North American Gamebird Association advocates for and supports those who raise and hunt for game birds. The non-profit organization works to improve methods of game bird

production and in managing hunting land. It also holds an annual convention, at which educational components are offered.

Western Gamebird Alliance
PO Box 14152
Tucson, AZ 85732
(520) 241-3534
info@gamebird-alliance.org
http://www.gamebird-alliance.org

The Western Gamebird Alliance is a non-profit organization that works to restore gamebird habitats in the western part of the United States. It lobbies to have a say in land management, and encourages its members to support causes and legislation that are favorable to the interests of bird hunters.

GAME WARDEN

North American Game Warden Museum
PO Box 28
Valley City, ND 58072-0028
(701) 845-3780
http://www.gamewardenmuseum.org/index.php

The Game Warden Museum will feature a range of programs, exhibits, and other resources, all with the goal of celebrating natural resource protection.

North American Wildlife Enforcement Officers Association (NAWEOA)
http://www.naweoa.org/mod.php?mod=userpage&page_id=26

NAWEOA is an 8,000-member organization of wildlife and fisheries enforcement officers from across North America. NAWEOA supports the activities of many major conservation organizations through membership and active participation.

HIKING TRAIL DESIGNER

New York–New Jersey Trail Conference
156 Ramapo Valley Road
Mahway, NJ 07430
(201) 512-9348
info@nynjtc.org
http://www.nynjtc.org

This federation of more than 85 hiking clubs and environmental organizations and 10,000 individuals dedicated to building and maintaining marked hiking trails and protecting related open space in the bi-state region.

INSECT CONTROL TECHNICIAN

Entomological Society of America
10001 Derekwood Lane, Suite 100
Lanham, MD 20706-4876
(301) 731-4535
http://www.entsoc.org

The Entomological Society of America is a resource, advocate, and source of education and information for entomologists and those interested in the field of entomology. It offers educational training, seminars, and other resources for its members, which number 6,000. The organization offers online journals and newsletters, and links to other, related Web sites.

National Pest Management Association, Inc. (NPMA)
8100 Oak Street
Dunn Loring, VA 22027
(703) 573-8330
http://www.pestworld.com

The National Pest Management Association has been operating for more than 60 years to serve as a voice for insect control operators and educate consumers about the benefits of pest control. Its Web site has news for consumers and professionals, links to related sites and an online store.

IRRIGATION SPECIALIST

The Irrigation Association
6540 Arlington Boulevard
Falls Church, VA 22042-6638
(703) 536-7080
http://www.irrigation.org

The Irrigation Association has been working since 1949 to promote and achieve water conservation through effective irrigation. A nonprofit orginization, it supports the irrigation industry, provides education and training, informs consumers about the potential benefits of irrigation, and advocates for irrigation companies and firms.

LANDSCAPE DESIGNER

The Association of Professional Landscape Designers (APLD)
1924 North Second Street
Harrisburg, PA 17102
(717) 238-9780
http://www.apld.com

This association was formed to increase recognition of landscape design as an independent profession and to promote landscape designers as highly qualified, dedicated professionals. The Web site contains member lists and other information.

Lawn and Landscape
http://www.lawnandlandscape.com

A comprehensive Web site for the lawn and landscape industry, containing information about the state of the industry, cost of business, new products and where they are available, landscape associations, news relevant to the landscape industry, and more.

MAPLE SYRUP PRODUCER

**Massachusetts Maple
Producers Association**
Watson-Spruce Corner Road
Ashfield, MA 01330
(413) 628-3912
http://www.massmaple.org

A nonprofit organization that works to promote and preserve maple sugaring in its state, the Massachusetts Maple Producers Association Web site is loaded with information about maple syrup, the business of sugaring, locations of sugarhouses within the state, and links to many other sites.

Proctor Maple Research Center
PO Box 233, Harvey Road
Underhill Center, VT 05490
(802) 899-9926
http://www.uvm.edu/~pmrc

The center conducts a variety of research concerning the production of maple syrup; provides educational opportunities for producers, students, and other interested people; and demonstrates how maple syrup is made. Anyone interested can schedule a tour or a presentation by a representative of the center.

MUSHROOM GROWER

American Mushroom Institute (AMI)
One Massachusetts Avenue, NW,
Suite 800
Washington, DC 20001
(202) 842-4344

ami@mwmlaw.com
http://www.americanmushroom.org

The Mushroom Council
11501 Dublin Boulevard, Suite 200
Dublin, CA 94568
(925) 558-2749
info@mushroomcouncil.org
http://www.mushroomcouncil.org

**National Future Farmers of America
(FFA) Organization**
The National FFA Center
Career Information Requests
PO Box 68690
Indianapolis, IN 46268-0960
http://www.ffa.org

The New England Small Farm Institute
275 Jackson Street
Belchertown, MA 01007
http://smallfarm.org

ORCHARD OPERATOR

Fruit Growers News
Great American Publishing
75 Applewood Drive, Suite A
PO Box 128
Sparta, MI 49345
(616) 887-9008
http://www.fruitgrowersnews.com

Published monthly, the Fruit Growers News *is a tabloid-sized publication that includes timely issues and topics of concern to fruit growers across the nation. It also features successful fruit growing operations and columns by university and extension specialists.*

ORGANIC FARM MANAGER

**The Center for Agroecology
and Sustainable Food Systems**

University of California, Santa Cruz
1156 High Street
Santa Cruz, CA 95064
(831) 459-3240
http://zzyx.ucsc.edu/casfs/index.html

*A research facility of the University of
California at Santa Cruz, the Center
for Agroecology and Sustainable Food
Systems is widely recognized for its work
to advance and develop sustainable food
and agricultural systems using organic
methods. The center collaborates with
organizations ranging from small farms
to the U.S. Department of Agriculture
to advance its research. It also offers
education and some internships. The
center's on-campus farm is open daily
from 8 a.m. until 6 p.m.*

OYSTER SHUCKER

Southern Maryland Online
http://www.somd.com

*An illustrated explanation of how to
shuck an oyster is provided on this
Web site, along with links to St. Mary's
County's annual oyster festival Web
site and other information concerning
oysters. Click on the "dining" link of the
Web site, and then on "How to Shuck
an Oyster."*

PARK RANGER

**Association of National
Park Rangers (ANPR)**
PO Box 108
Larned, KS 67550
http://www.anpr.org

*For more than 27 years ANPR has
communicated for, about, and with park
rangers; promoted and enhanced the park*

*ranger profession and its spirit; supported
management and the perpetuation of the
National Park Service and the National
Park System; and provided a forum
for social enrichment. The association
provides education and other training to
develop the skills of rangers and provides
information to the public.*

**National Association
of State Park Directors**
9894 East Holden Place
Tuscon, AZ 85748
(520) 298-4924
http://naspd.indstate.edu

**National Recreation
and Park Association**
22377 Belmont Ridge Road
Ashburn, VA 20148
(703) 858-4730
http://www.activeparks.org

PEANUT FARMER

American Peanut Council (APC)
1500 King Street, Suite 301
Alexandria, VA 22314
http://www.peanutsusa.com

*The American Peanut Council (APC)
is the trade association that represents
all segments of the peanut industry.
Members include peanut growers,
peanut shellers, brokers, peanut product
manufacturers, and suppliers of goods
and services to the industry.*

The National Agricultural Library
10301 Baltimore Avenue, Room 132
Beltsville, MD 20705
http://www.nal.usda.gov

*For information on a wide range of
topics in agriculture, contact the library
at the above Web site.*

National Peanut Board
900 Circle 75 Parkway Suite 1220
Atlanta, GA 30339
(866) 825-7946
http://www.nationalpeanutboard.org

A research and promotion board that works on behalf of all U.S. peanut farmers to support and expand existing markets, develop new markets, and facilitate the economical production of high-quality, USA peanuts for consumers worldwide.

Small Farm Program
U.S. Department of Agriculture
Cooperative State, Research,
Education, and Extension Service
Stop 2215
Washington, DC 20250
http://www.usda.gov/oce/smallfarm

For general information about farming and agricultural occupations, contact the government's Small Farm Program.

RANGE MANAGER

Behavioral Education for Human, Animal, Vegetation, & Ecosystem Management (BEHAVE)
http://www.behave.net

A consortium that works together to inspire people to master and apply behavioral principles in managing ecosystems. Consortium members include Utah State University, University of Arizona, University of Idaho, Montana State University, National Wildlife Research Center, and an advisory board of 40 people from throughout the United States.

Society for Range Management (SRM)
445 Union Boulevard, Suite 230
Lakewood, CO 80228

http://www.rangelands.org/
ScriptContent/Index.cfm

Web site offers information about a career as a range manager, as well as a list of schools offering training.

TIMBER HARVESTER

Timber West Journal
PO Box 610
300 Admiral Way, Suite #208
Edmonds, WA 98020
(425) 778-3388
http://www.forestnet.com/timberwest

Published each month by Timber/West Publications, the journal is geared toward loggers and lumber producers in the western part of the United States. Topics addressed in the magazine include logging techniques, equipment, industry news, legislative issues, people within the industry, and more.

TOPIARY GARDENER

The Association of Professional Landscape Designers (APLD)
1924 North Second Street
Harrisburg, PA 17102
(717) 238-9780
http://www.apld.com

This association was formed to increase recognition of landscape design, including topiary gardening, as an independent profession and to promote landscape designers as highly qualified, dedicated professionals. The Web site contains member lists and other information.

Lawn and Landscape
http://www.lawnandlandscape.com

A comprehensive Web site for the lawn and landscape industry, containing information about the state of the industry, cost of business, new products and where they are available, landscape associations, news relevant to the landscape industry, and more.

TURF SCIENTIST

Sports Turf Managers Association
http://www.sportsturfmanager.org

WINEGROWER (VITICULTURIST)

American Society for Enology & Viticulture–Eastern Section
ASEV/ES Food Science Building
Purdue University
West Lafayette, IN 47907-1160
(765) 494-6704
harkness@foodsci.purdue.edu
http://www.nysaes.cornell.edu/fst/faculty/henick/asev

This organization provides discussions on research and technology for the advancement of wines and solving problems of special interest to the enology and viticulture of grapes grown in the Eastern United States and Canada. The geographical area included in this organization includes all states east of the western borders of Minnesota, Iowa, Missouri, Arkansas, and Louisiana, plus the Canadian Provinces east of the Ontario-Manitoba border.

American Vineyard Foundation (AVF)
Box 5779
Napa, CA 94581
(707) 252-6911
http://www.avf.org

A California corporation organized in 1978 by the American Society of Enology and Viticulture as a vehicle to raise funds for research in viticulture and enology. Basic and applied research has made the American grape and wine industry the world's leader. Our vineyards produce grapes of unsurpassed quantity and quality.

Benchmark Consulting: Wine Positions
103 East Napa Street, Suite 1
Sonoma, CA 95476
(707) 933-1500
http://www.winecareers.com

Napa Valley Vintners Association
PO Box 141
Saint Helena, CA 94574
(707) 963-3388
http://www.napavintners.com

Founded in 1943, the organization is a regional trade association with an active membership of 222 wineries, representing a tradition of dedicated vintners and grape growers who have worked and cared for this premier winegrowing region since the early 1800s.

APPENDIX B: ONLINE CAREER RESOURCES

This volume offers a look inside a wide range of unusual and unique careers that might appeal to someone who loves working outdoors, either in nature or some type of agriculture. While this book highlights general information about each job, it's really only a glimpse into these unusual careers. The entries are intended to merely whet your appetite, and provide you with some career options you maybe never knew existed.

Before jumping into any career, you'll want to do more research to make sure that it's really something you want to pursue. This way, as you continue to do research and talk to experts in particular fields, you can ask informed and intelligent questions that will help you make your decisions. You might want to research the education options for learning the skills you'll need to be successful, along with scholarships, work-study programs, and other opportunities to help you finance that education. And you might want answers to questions that were not addressed in the information provided here. If you search long enough, you can find just about anything on the Internet, including additional information about the jobs featured in this book.

* **A word about Internet safety:** The Internet is a wonderful resource for networking. Many job and career sites have forums where students can interact with others working in those fields. Some sites offer online chat rooms where visitors can interact with each other. This provides students and job seekers opportunities to make connections and begin to establish some contacts to help with future employment.

These days, most students learn about Internet safety in school computer classes. But we want to emphasize safety issues here: As you visit these forums and chat rooms, remember that anyone could be on the other side of that computer screen telling you exactly what you want to hear. It's easy to get wrapped up in the excitement of the moment when you're in a forum or a chat, interacting with people who share your career dreams. Be cautious about what kind of personal information you make available on the forums and in the chats; never give out your full name, address, or phone number. And never agree to meet with someone you've met online.

SEARCH ENGINES

When looking for information, there are many search engines you could use besides the well-known Google to help you find out more about adventurous jobs. You may already have a favorite search engine, but you might want to take some time to check out some of the others. Some have features that might help you find information you couldn't locate anywhere else. Several engines offer suggestions for ways to narrow your results, or suggest related phrases you might want to use. This is handy if you are having trouble locating exactly what you want.

It's also a good idea to learn how to use the advanced search features of your favorite search engines. Knowing the advanced possibilities might help you to zero-in on exactly the information for which you're searching without wasting time looking through pages of irrelevant hits.

As you use the Internet to search information on the perfect career, keep in mind that like anything you find on the Internet, you need to consider the source from which the information comes.

Some of the most popular Internet search engines are:

AllSearchEngines.com
http://www.allsearchengines.com
This search engine index has links to the major search engines along with search engines grouped by topic. The site includes a page with more than 75 career and job search engines at http:// allsearchengines.com/careerjobs.html.

AlltheWeb
http://www.alltheweb.com

AltaVista
http://www.altavista.com

Ask.com
http://www.ask.com

Dogpile
http://www.dogpile.com

Excite
http://www.excite.com

Google
http://www.google.com

HotBot
http://www.hotbot.com

LookSmart
http://www.looksmart.com

Lycos
http://www.lycos.com

Mamma.com
http://www.mamma.com

MSN Network
http://www.msn.com

My Way
http://www.goto.com

Teoma
http://www.directhit.com

Vivisimo
http://www.vivisimo.com

Yahoo!
http://www.yahoo.com

HELPFUL WEB SITES

The Internet has a wealth of information on careers—everything from the mundane to the outrageous. There are thousands, if not millions, of sites devoted to helping you find the perfect job for you; and your interests, skills, and talents. The sites listed here are some of the most helpful ones we've found while researching the jobs in this volume. These sites, which are listed in alphabetical order, are offered for your information. The authors do not endorse any of the information found on these sites.

All Experts
http://www.allexperts.com
"The oldest & largest free Q&A service on the Internet," AllExperts.com has thousands of volunteer experts to answer

your questions. You can also read replies to questions asked by other people. Each expert has an online profile to help you pick someone who might be best suited to answer your question. Very easy to use, it's a great resource for finding experts who can help to answer your questions.

America's Career InfoNet
http://www.acinet.org

A wealth of information! You can get a feel for the general job market; check out wages and trends in a particular state for different jobs; learn more about the knowledge, skills, abilities, and tasks for specific careers; and learn about required certifications for specific careers and how to get them. You can search over 5,000 scholarship and other financial opportunities to help you further your education. A huge career resources library has links to nearly 6,500 online resources. And for fun, you can take a break and watch one of nearly 450 videos featuring real people at work.

Backdoor Jobs: Short-Term Job Adventures, Summer Jobs, Volunteer Vacations, Work Abroad, and More
http://www.backdoorjobs.com

This is the Web site of the popular book by the same name, now in its third edition. While not as extensive as the book, the site still offers a wealth of information for people looking for short-term opportunities: internships, seasonal jobs, volunteer vacations, and work abroad situations. Job opportunities are classified into several categories: Adventure Jobs, Camps, Ranches & Resort Jobs, Ski Resort Jobs, Jobs in the Great Outdoors, Nature Lover Jobs, Sustainable Living and Farming Work,

Artistic & Learning Adventures, Heart Work, and Opportunities Abroad.

Boston Works–Job Explainer
http://bostonworks.boston.com/globe/job_explainer/archive.html

For nearly 18 months, the Boston Globe ran a weekly series profiling a wide range of careers. Some of the jobs were more traditional, but with a twist, like the veterinarian who makes house calls. Others were very unique and unusual, like the profile of a Superior of Society monk. The profiles discuss an average day, challenges of the job, required training, salary, and more. Each profile gives an up-close and personal look at that particular career. In addition, the Boston Works Web site (http://bostonworks.boston.com) has a lot of good, general employment-related information.

Career Guide to Industries
http://www.bls.gov/oco/cg/cgindex.htm

For someone interested in working in a specific industry, but maybe undecided about exactly what career to pursue, this site is the place to start. Put together by the U.S. Department of Labor, you can learn more about the industry, working conditions, employment, occupations (in the industry), training and advancement, earnings, outlook, and sources of additional information.

Career Planning at About.com
http://careerplanning.about.com

Like most of the other About.com topics, the career-planning area offers a wealth of information, and links to other information on the Web. Among the excellent essentials are career planning A to Z, a career-planning glossary, information on career choices, and a free career-planning class. There are many great articles and other excellent resources.

Career Prospects in Virginia

http://www3.ccps.virginia.edu/career_prospects/default-search.html

Career Prospects is a database of entries with information about more than 400 careers. Developed by the Virginia Career Resource Network, the online career information resource of the Virginia Department of Education, Office of Career and Technical Education Services, was intended as a source of information about jobs "important to Virginia," but it's actually a great source of information for anyone. While some of the information like wages, outlook, and some of the requirements may apply only to Virginia, the other information for each job (such as what it's like, getting ahead, skills) and the links will be of help to anyone interested in that career.

Career Voyages

http://www.careervoyages.gov

"The ultimate road trip to career success," sponsored by the U.S. Department of Labor and the U.S. Department of Education. This site features sections for students, parents, career changers, and career advisors with information and resources aimed to that specific group. The FAQ offers great information about getting started, the high-growth industries, how to find your perfect job, how to make sure you're qualified for the job you want, tips for paying for the training and education you need, and more. Also interesting are the hot careers and the emerging fields.

Dream Jobs

http://www.salary.com/careers/layouthtmls/crel_display_Cat10.html

The staff at Salary.com takes a look at some wild, wacky, outrageous, and totally cool ways to earn a living. The jobs they highlight include pro skateboarder, computer game guru, nose, diplomat, and much more. The profiles don't offer links or resources for more information, but they are informative and fun to read.

Find It! in DOL

http://www.dol.gov/dol/findit.htm

A handy source for finding information at the extensive U.S. Department of Labor Web site. You can search by broad topic category or by audience, which includes a section for students.

Fine Living: *Radical Sabbatical*

http://www.fineliving.com/fine/episode_archive/0,1663,FINE_1413_14,00.html#Series873

The show Radical Sabbatical *on the Fine Living network looks at people willing to take a chance and follow their dreams and passions. The show focuses on individuals between the ages of 20 and 65 who have made the decision to leave successful, lucrative careers to start over, usually in an unconventional career. You can read all about these people and their journeys on the show's Web site.*

Free Salary Survey Reports and Cost of Living Reports

http://www.salaryexpert.com

Based on information from a number of sources, Salary Expert will tell you what kind of salary you can expect to make for a certain job in a certain geographic location. Salary Expert has information

on hundreds of jobs; everything from
your more traditional white- and
blue-collar jobs, to some unique and
out of the ordinary professions like
acupressurist, blacksmith, denture
waxer, taxidermist, and many others.
With sections covering schools, crime,
community comparison, community
explorer, and more, the Moving Center
is a useful area for people who need to
relocate for training or employment.

Fun Jobs
http://www.funjobs.com

Fun Jobs has job listings for adventure,
outdoor, and fun jobs at ranches, camps,
ski resorts, and more. The job postings
have a lot of information about the
position, requirements, benefits, and
responsibilities so that you know what
you are getting into ahead of time. And,
you can apply online for most of the
positions. The Fun Companies link will
let you look up companies in an A-to-Z
listing, or you can search for companies
in a specific area or by keyword.
The company listings offer you more
detailed information about the location,
types of jobs available, employment
qualifications, and more.

Girls Can Do
http://www.girlscando.com

"Helping girls discover their life's
passions," Girls Can Do has
opportunities, resources, and a lot
of other cool stuff for girls ages 8 to
18. Girls can explore sections such as
Outdoor Adventure, Sports, My Body,
The Arts, Sci-Tech, Change the World,
and Learn, Earn, and Intern. In addition
to reading about women in all sorts of
careers, girls can explore a wide range of

opportunities and information that will
help them grow into strong, intelligent,
capable women.

Great Web Sites for Kids
http://www.ala.org/gwstemplate.cfm?se
ction=greatwebsites&template=/cfapps/
gws/default.cfm

Great Web Sites for Kids is a collection
of more than 700 sites organized into a
variety of categories, including animals,
sciences, the arts, reference, social
sciences, and more. All of the sites
included here have been approved by
a committee made up of professional
librarians and educators. You can even
submit your favorite "great site" for
possible inclusion.

Hot Jobs: Career Tools
http://www.hotjobs.com/htdocs/tools/
index-us.html

While the jobs listed at Hot Jobs are
more on the traditional side, the Career
Tools area has a lot of great resources
for anyone looking for a job. You'll find
information about how to write a resume
and a cover letter, how to put together a
career portfolio, interviewing tips, links
to career assessments, and much more.

Job Descriptions & Job Details
http://www.job-descriptions.org

Search for descriptions and details for
more than 13,000 jobs at this site. You
can search for jobs by category or by
industry. You'd probably be hard-pressed
to find a job that isn't listed here, and
you'll probably find lots of jobs you
never imagined existed. The descriptions
and details are short, but it's interesting
and fun, and might lead you to the career
of your dreams.

Job Hunter's Bible

http://www.jobhuntersbible.com

This site is the official online supplement to the book What Color Is Your Parachute? A Practical Manual for Job-Hunters and Career-Changers, *and is a great source of information with lots of informative, helpful articles and links to many more resources.*

Job Profiles

http://www.jobprofiles.org

A collection of profiles in which experienced workers share rewards of their job, stressful parts of their job, basic skills the job demands, challenges of the future, and advice on entering the field. The careers include everything from baseball ticket manager to pastry chef and much, much more. The hundreds of profiles are arranged by broad category. While most of the profiles are easy to read, you can check out the How to browse JobProfiles.org section (http://www.jobprofiles.org/jphowto.htm) if you have any problems.

Major Job Web sites at Careers.org

http://www.careers.org/topic/01_jobs_10.html

This page at the Careers.org Web site has links for more than 40 of the Web's major job-related Web sites. While you're there, check out the numerous links to additional information.

Monster Jobs

http://www.monster.com

Monster.com is one of the largest, and probably best known, job resource sites on the Web. It's really one-stop shopping for almost anything job-related that you can imagine. You can find a new job, network, update your resume, improve your skills, plan a job change or relocation, and so much more. Of special interest are the Monster: Cool Careers (http://change.monster.com/archives/coolcareers) and the Monster: Job Profiles (http://jobprofiles.monster.com) sections, where you can read about some really neat careers. The short profiles also include links to additional information. The Monster: Career Advice section (http://content.monster.com) has resume and interviewing advice, message boards where you can network, relocation tools and advice, and more.

Occupational Outlook Handbook

http://www.bls.gov/oco

Published by the U.S. Department of Labor's Bureau of Labor Statistics, the Occupational Outlook Handbook *(sometimes referred to as the* OOH*) is the premiere source of career information. The book is updated every two years, so you can be assured that the information you are using to help make your decisions is current. The online version is very easy to use; you can search for a specific occupation, browse though a group of related occupations, or look through an alphabetical listing of all the jobs included in the volume. Each of the entries highlights the general nature of the job, working conditions, training and other qualifications, job outlook, average earning, related occupations, and sources of additional information. Each entry covers several pages and is a terrific source to get some great information about a huge variety of jobs.*

The Riley Guide: Employment Opportunities and Job Resources on the Internet
http://www.rileyguide.com

The Riley Guide is an amazing collection of job and career resources. Unless you are looking for something specific, one of the best ways to maneuver around the site is with the A-to-Z Index. You can find everything from links to careers in enology to information about researching companies and employers. The Riley Guide is a great place to find just about anything you might be looking for, and probably lots of things you aren't looking for. But be forewarned—it's easy to get lost in the A-to-Z Index, reading about all sorts of interesting things.

USA TODAY Career Focus
http://www.usatoday.com/careers/dream/dreamarc.htm

Several years ago, USA TODAY ran a series featuring people working in their dream jobs. In the profiles, people discuss how they got their dream job, what they enjoy the most about it, they talk about an average day, their education backgrounds, sacrifices they had to make for their jobs, and more. They also share words of advice for anyone hoping to follow in their footsteps. Most of the articles also feature links where you can find more information. The USATODAY. com Job Center (http://www.usatoday. com/money/jobcenter/front.htm) also has links to lots of resources and additional information.

CAREER TESTS AND INVENTORIES

If you have no idea what career is right for you, there are many resources available online that will help assess your interests and maybe steer you in the right direction. While some of the assessments charge a fee, there are many out there that are free. You can locate more tests and inventories by searching for the keywords *career tests*, *career inventories*, or *personality inventories*. Some of the most popular assessments available online are:

Campbell Interest and Skill Survey (CISS)
http://www.usnews.com/usnews/edu/careers/ccciss.htm

Career Explorer
http://careerexplorer.net/aptitude.asp

Career Focus 2000 Interest Inventory
http://www.iccweb.com/careerfocus

Career Maze
http://www.careermaze.com/home.asp?licensee=CareerMaze

Career Tests at CareerPlanner.com
http://www.careerplanner.com

CAREERLINK Inventory
http://www.mpc.edu/cl/cl.htm

FOCUS
http://www.focuscareer.com

Keirsey Temperament Test
http://www.keirsey.com

Motivational Appraisal of Personal Potential (MAPP)
http://www.assessment.com

Myers-Briggs Personality Type
http://www.personalitypathways.com/type_inventory.html

Skills Profiler
http://www.acinet.org/acinet/skills_home.asp

The Career Interests Game
http://career.missouri.edu/students/
explore/thecareerinterestsgame.php

The Career Key
http://www.careerkey.org

Princeton Review Career Quiz
http://www.princetonreview.com/cte/
quiz/default.asp

APPENDIX C: AGRICULTURAL COLLEGES AND UNIVERSITIES

The country's first colleges to specialize in teaching agriculture were the series of land-grant colleges that were set up as a result of the Morrill Acts of 1862 and 1890, signed into law by Abraham Lincoln and Benjamin Harrison, respectively. The original mission of these colleges was to teach agriculture, among other things, so that members of the working classes could obtain a liberal, practical education. A key part of the land-grant system is the agricultural experiment station program created by the Hatch Act of 1887, which provides for federal grant funds to be paid to each state each year through a formula based on the number of small farmers there. To publish information gleaned from the experiment stations' research, the Smith-Lever Act of 1914 created a Cooperative Extension Service also associated with each land-grant school.

Passage of the first Morrill Act in 1862 reflected a growing demand for agricultural and technical education in the United States. While a number of institutions had begun to expand upon the traditional classical curriculum, higher education was still widely unavailable to many agricultural and industrial workers. The Morrill Act was intended to provide a broad segment of the population with a practical education that had direct relevance to their daily lives.

There is now at least one land-grant school in every state; some southern states have two land-grant schools as a result of the second Morrill Act of 1890, and some western and plains states have several of the 1994 land-grant tribal colleges.

ALABAMA

Alabama Agricultural and Mechanical University
4900 Meridian Street
Huntsville, AL 35811
(256) 372-5000
http://www.aamu.edu

Auburn University
Auburn, AL 36849
(334) 844-4000
http://www.auburn.edu

Tuskegee University
102 Old Admin Building
Tuskegee, AL 36088
(800) 622- 6531
http://www.tuskegee.edu

ALASKA

University of Alaska Fairbanks
PO Box 757500
Fairbanks, AK 99775
(907) 474-7211
http://www.uaf.edu

ARIZONA

University of Arizona
The University of Arizona

Tucson, AZ 85721
(520) 621-2211
http://www.arizona.edu

ARKANSAS

University of Arkansas
Fayetteville, AR 72701
(479) 575-2000
http://www.uark.edu

University of Arkansas at Pine Bluff
1200 N. University Drive
Pine Bluff, AR 71601
(870) 575-8000
http://www.uapb.edu

CALIFORNIA

University of California, Davis
One Shields Avenue
Davis, CA 95616
(530) 752-1011
http://www.ucdavis.edu

University of California, Riverside
900 University Avenue
Riverside, CA 92521
(951) 827-1012
http://www.ucr.edu

COLORADO

Colorado State University
Fort Collins, CO 80523
(970) 491-1101
http://www.colostate.edu

CONNECTICUT

University of Connecticut
Storrs, CT 06269

(860) 486-2000
http://www.uconn.edu

DELAWARE

Delaware State University
1200 North DuPont Highway
Dover, DE 19901
(302) 857-6060
http://www.desu.edu

University of Delaware
Newark, DE 19716
(302) 831-2791
http://www.udel.edu

DISTRICT OF COLUMBIA

University of the District of Columbia
4200 Connecticut Avenue, NW
Washington, DC 20008
(202) 274-5000
http://www.universityofdc.org

FLORIDA

Florida A&M University
Tallahassee, FL 32307
(850) 599-3000
http://www.famu.edu

University of Florida
Gainesville, FL 32611
(352)392-3261
http://www.ufl.edu

GEORGIA

University of Georgia
Athens, GA 30602
(706) 542-3000
http://www.uga.edu

GUAM

University of Guam
UOG Station Mangilao, GU 96923
(671) 735-2291
http://www.ug.edu

HAWAII

University of Hawaii at Manoa
2500 Campus Road, Hawaii Hall 202
Honolulu, HI 96822
(808) 956-8111
http://www.uhm.edu

IDAHO

University of Idaho
921 South 8th Avenue
Pocatello, ID 83209
(208) 282-0211
http://www.isu.edu

ILLINOIS

University of Illinois at Urbana-Champaign
1401 West Green Street
Urbana, IL 61801
(217) 333-4666
http://www.uiuc.edu

INDIANA

Purdue University
1533 Stewart Center
West Lafayette, IN 47907-1533.
(765) 494-4600
http://www.purdue.edu

IOWA

Iowa State University
Ames, IA 50011
(515) 294-4111
http://www.iastate.edu

KANSAS

Kansas State University
Manhattan, KS 66506
(785) 532-6011
http://www.ku.edu

KENTUCKY

University of Kentucky
Lexington, KY 40506
(859) 257-9000
http://www.uky.edu

LOUISIANA

Louisiana State University
Baton Rouge, LA 70803
(225) 578-1175
http://www.lsu.edu

MAINE

University of Maine
Orono, ME 04469
(207) 581-1110
http://www.umaine.edu

MARYLAND

University of Maryland, College Park
College Park, MD 20742

(301) 405-1000
http://www.umd.edu

University of Maryland, Eastern Shore
1 Backbone Road
Princess Anne, MD 21853
(410) 651-2200
http://www.umes.edu

MASSACHUSETTS

University of Massachusetts, Amherst
Amherst, MA 01003
(413) 545-0111
http://www.umass.edu

MICHIGAN

Alcorn State University
1000 ASU Drive
Alcorn State, MI 39096
(601) 877-6100
http://www.alcorn.edu

Michigan State University
250 Administration Building
East Lansing, MI 48824-0590
(517) 355-8332
http://admissions.msu.edu/ContactUs.asp

MINNESOTA

University of Minnesota, Twin Cities
240 Williamson Hall
231 Pillsbury Drive S.E.
Minneapolis, MN 55455-0213

(612) 625-5000
http://www.umn.edu

MISSISSIPPI

Mississippi State University
Mississippi State, MS 39762
(662) 325-2323
http://www.msstate.edu

MISSOURI

Lincoln University (Missouri)
820 Chestnut Street
Jefferson City, MO 65101
(800) 521-5052
http://www.lincolnu.edu

University of Missouri–Columbia
Columbia, MO 65211
(573) 882-2121
http://www.missouri.edu

NEBRASKA

University of Nebraska–Lincoln
332 Canfield Administration Building
Lincoln, NE 68588
(402) 472-7211
http://www.unl.edu/unlpub/index.shtml

NEVADA

University of Nevada, Reno
1664 North Virginia Street

Reno, NV 89557-0042
(775) 784-1110
http://www.unr.edu/content

NEW HAMPSHIRE

University of New Hampshire
Office of Admissions, Grant House
4 Garrison Avenue
Durham, NH 03824
(603) 862-1234
http://www.unh.edu/admissions

NEW JERSEY

Rutgers University
83 Somerset Street
New Brunswick, NJ 08901
(732) 932-4636
http://www.rutgers.edu

NEW MEXICO

New Mexico State University
PO Box 30001
Las Cruces, NM 88003-8001
(505) 646-0111
http://www.nmsu.edu

NEW YORK

Cornell University
Ithaca, NY 14853
http://www.cornell.edu

NORTH CAROLINA

North Carolina Agricultural and
Technical State University
1601 East Market Street
Greensboro NC 27411
(336) 334-7500
http://www.ncat.edu

North Carolina State University
Box 7005
Raleigh, NC 27695
(919) 515-2011
http://www.ncsu.edu

NORTH DAKOTA

North Dakota State University
1301 12th Avenue North
Fargo, ND 58105
(701) 231-8643
http://www.ndsu.edu

OHIO

Ohio State University
111 Bricker Hall
190 North Oval Mall
Columbus, OH 43210
(614) 292-OHIO
http://www.osu.edu

OKLAHOMA

Langston University
PO Box 1600

Langston, OK 73050
(405) 466-3292
http://www.lunet.edu

Oklahoma State University–Stillwater
219 Student Union
Stillwater, OK 74078-1012
(800) 852-1255
http://osu.okstate.edu

OREGON

Oregon State University
646 Kerr Administration Building
Corvallis, OR 97331-4501
(541) 737-1000
http://oregonstate.edu

PENNSYLVANIA

Pennsylvania State University
201 Shields Building
Box 3000
University Park, PA 16804-3000
(814) 865-5471
http://www.psu.edu

RHODE ISLAND

University of Rhode Island
Kingston, RI 02881
(401) 874-1000
http://www.uri.edu

SOUTH CAROLINA

Clemson University
Clemson, SC 29634

(864) 656-3311
http://www.clemson.edu

South Carolina State University
PO Box 7127
300 College Street, NE
Orangeburg, SC 29117-0001
(803) 536-7185
http://www.scsu.edu

SOUTH DAKOTA

South Dakota State University
ADM 310
PO Box 2201
Brookings, SD 57007
(800) 952-3541
http://www3.sdstate.edu

TENNESSEE

Tennessee State University
Post Office Box 9609
John A. Merritt Boulevard
Nashville, TN 37209-1561
(888) 463-6878
http://www.tnstate.edu

University of Tennessee
711 Andy Holt Tower
Knoxville, TN 37996-0174
(865) 974-2243
http://www.utk.edu

TEXAS

Prairie View A&M University
PO Box 519
Prairie View, TX 77446-0519

(936) 857-3311
http://www.pvamu.edu

UTAH

Utah State University
0160 Old Main Hill
Logan, UT 84322
(435) 797-1000
http://www.usu.edu

VERMONT

University of Vermont
194 South Prospect Street
Burlington, VT 05405
(802) 656-3131
http://www.uvm.edu

VIRGINIA

**Virginia Polytechnic Institute
and State University**
201 Burruss Hall
Blacksburg, VA 24061
(540) 231-6000
http://www.vt.edu

Virginia State University
Petersburg, VA 23806
(804) 524-5000
http://www.vsu.edu

WASHINGTON

Washington State University
Lighty 370
Pullman, WA 99164-1067
(888) 468-6978
http://www.wsu.edu

WEST VIRGINIA

West Virginia University
Institute, WV
(800) 987-2112
http://www.wvsc.edu

WISCONSIN

University of Wisconsin–Madison
716 Langdon Street
Madison, WI 53706-1481
(608) 262–3961
http://www.wisc.edu

WYOMING

University of Wyoming
1000 East University Avenue
Laramie, WY 82071
(307) 766-1121
http://www.uwyo.edu

READ MORE ABOUT IT

The following sources and books may help you learn more about careers in agriculture and nature.

GENERAL CAREERS

Camenson, Blythe. *Real People Working in Service Businesses*. Lincolnwood, Ill.: VGM Career Horizons, 1997.

Culbreath, Alice N., and Saundra K. Neal. *Testing the Waters: A Teen's Guide to Career Exploration*. New York: JRC Consulting, 1999.

Doyle, Kevin. *The Complete Guide to Environmental Careers in the 21st Century*. Washington, D.C.: Island Press, 1998.

Farr, Michael, LaVerne L. Ludden, and Laurence Shatkin. *200 Best Jobs for College Graduates*. Indianapolis, Ind.: Jist Publishing, 2003.

Fasulo, Mike, and Jane Kinney. *Careers for Environmental Types & Others Who Respect the Earth*. New York: McGraw-Hill, 2001.

Fogg, Neeta, Paul Harrington, and Thomas Harrington. *College Majors Handbook with Real Career Paths and Payoffs: The Actual Jobs, Earnings, and Trends for Graduates of 60 College Majors*. Indianapolis, Ind.: Jist Publishing, 2004.

Hiam, Alex, and Susan Angle. *Adventure Careers: Your Guide to Exciting Jobs, Uncommon Occupations and Extraordinary Experiences*. 2nd ed. Franklin Lakes, N.J.: Career Press, 1995.

Jakubiak, Joyce, ed. *Specialty Occupational Outlook: Trade and Technical*. Detroit: Gale Research, Inc., 1996.

Kains, M.G. *Five Acres and Independence: A Handbook for Small Farm Management*. New York: Dover Publications.

Krannich, Ronald L., and Caryl Rae Krannich. *The Best Jobs for the 1990s and into the 21st Century*. Manassas Park, Va.: Impact Publications, 1995.

Macher, Ron. Making Your Small Farm Profitable. North Adams, Mass.: Storey Books, 1999.

Mannion, James. *The Everything Alternative Careers Book: Leave the Office Behind and Embark on a New Adventure*. Boston: Adams, 2004.

Miller, Louise. *Careers for Nature Lovers & Other Outdoor Types*. New York: McGraw-Hill, 2001.

Minnesota Institute for Sustainable Agriculture. *Building a Sustainable Business: A Guide to Developing a Business Plan for Farms and Rural Businesses*. (Sustainable Agriculture Network Handbook Series, Bk. 6). Washington, DC: Sustainable Agriculture Network, 2003.

Quintana, Debra. *100 Jobs in the Environment*. New York: Macmillan, 1996.

Salatin, Joel F. *You Can Farm: The Entrepreneur's Guide to Start & Succeed in a Farming Enterprise*. Swope, Va.: Polyface, Inc., 1998.

Shenk, Ellen. *Outdoor Careers: Exploring Occupations in Outdoor Fields*. Mechanicsburg, Pa.: Stackpole Books, 2000.

U.S. Bureau of Labor Statistics. *Occupational Outlook Handbook*. 2006-07 ed. Available online at http://stats.bls.gov/search/ooh.asp?ct=OOH.

AGRONOMIST

Havlin, John L., and Samuel L. Tisdale. *Soil Fertility and Fertilizers: An Introduction to Nutrient Management.* 6th ed. New York: Prentice Hall, 1998.

Kinsey, Neal, and Charles Walters. *Neal Kinsey's Hands-On Agronomy.* Austin, Tex.: Acres USA, 1999.

ALPACA FARMER

Bennett, Marty McGee. *Llamas and Alpacas as a Metaphor for Life.* Dundee, N.Y.: Raccoon Press, 2003.

———. *The Camelid Companion.* Dundee, N.Y.: Raccoon Press, 2001.

Hoffman, Claire, and Ingrid Asmus. *Caring for Llamas and Alpacas: A Health & Management Guide.* Denver: Rocky Mountain Llama Association, 1996.

James, M. Brandon. *The Wonderful World of Alpacas.* Jackson, Calif.: Clay Press, 1997.

Schwenke, Karl. *Successful Small-Scale Farming: An Organic Approach.* North Adams, Mass.: Storey Books, 1991.

Smith, Bradford B. *Llama and Alpaca Neonatal Care.* Jackson, Calif.: Clay Press, 1996.

BEEKEEPER

Avitabile, Alphonse, and Diane Sammataro. *The Beekeeper's Handbook.* Ithaca, N.Y.: Cornell University Press, 1998.

Blackiston, Howland. *Beekeeping for Dummies.* New York: For Dummies, 2002.

Bonney, Richard E. *Hive Management: A Seasonal Guide for Beekeepers.* North Adams, Mass.: Storey Books, 1991.

Melzer, Werner, Walter Berghoff, and Matthew Vriends. *Beekeeping: A Practical Guide for the Novice Beekeeper Buying Bees, Management, Rearing, Honey Production/Special Section: The Beekeeper's Yearly Work Cycle.* Hauppauge, N.Y.: Barron's Educational Series, 1989.

Morse, Roger A. *The New Complete Guide to Beekeeping.* Woodstock, Vt.: Countryman Press, 1994.

Vivian, John. *Keeping Bees.* Charlotte, Vt.: Williamson Publishing Company, 1986.

BUG WRANGLER

Barner, Bob. *Bugs! Bugs! Bugs!* San Francisco: Chronicle Books, 1999.

Behlmer, Rudy. *America's Favorite Movies Behind the Scenes.* New York: Ungar Publishing Co., 1982.

Eastman, John. *Behind the Scenes of 500 Classic Movies.* New York: Ballantine Books, 1989.

Jackson, Donna M. *The Bug Scientists.* New York: Houghton Mifflin and Company, 2002.

Llewellyn, Claire. *The Best Book of Bugs.* Hyattsville, Md.: Kingfisher, 1998.

Mertins, James W. "Arthropods on the Screen." *Bulletin of the Entomological Society of America.* Summer 1986: 85-90.

Pallenberg, Barbara. *The Making of the Exorcist II: The Heretic.* New York: Warner Books, 1977.

Vaz, Mark Cotta. *Behind the Mask of Spider Man.* New York: Ballantine Publishing Group, 2002.

CHRISTMAS TREE GROWER

Albers, Henry, and Ann Kirk Davis. *Wonderful World of Christmas Trees.*

Parkersburg, Iowa: Mid-Prairie Books, 1997.

Beattie, Mollie, Charles Thompson, and Lynn Levine. *Working With Your Woodland: A Landowner's Guide.* Dartmouth, N.H.: University Press of New England, 1993.

Chapman, A.G. *Christmas Trees for Pleasure and Profit.* Piscataway, N.J.: Rutgers University Press, 1979.

Hill, Lewis. *Christmas Trees: Growing and Selling Trees, Wreaths and Greens.* Pownal, Vt.: Story Communications, Inc., 1991.

Hilts, Stewart, and Peter Mitchell. *The Woodlot Management Handbook: Making the Most of Your Wooded Property for Conservation, Income or Both.* Richmond Hill, Ontario: Firefly Books Ltd, 1999.

Morsbach, Hans W. *Common Sense Forestry.* White River Junction, Vt.: Chelsea Green Publishing Co., 2002.

Vardaman, James M. *How to Make Money Growing Trees.* New York: Wiley, 1989.

CITRUS GROWER

Vardaman, James M. *How to Make Money Growing Trees.* New York: Wiley, 1989.

CRAB FISHERMAN

Heitzmann, William Ray. *Opportunities in Marine And Maritime Careers.* New York: McGraw-Hill, 1999.

McCloskey, William. *Highliners: The Classic Novel about the Commercial Fishermen of Alaska.* The Lyons Press, 2000.

Walker, Spike. *Working on the Edge: Surviving in the World's Most Dangerous Profession—King Crab Fishing on Alaska's High Seas.* New York: St. Martin's Press, 1993.

———. *Nights of Ice.* New York: St. Martin's Press, 1999.

Warner, William W. *Beautiful Swimmers: Watermen, Crabs and the Chesapeake Bay.* Boston: Back Bay Books, 1994.

CRANBERRY FARMER

Trehane, Jennifer. *Blueberries, Cranberries, and Other Vacciniums.* Portland, Ore.: Timber Press, 2004.

CROP DUSTER

Rasmussen, Henry. *Props in the Crops.* Saint Paul, Minn.: Motorbooks International, 1986.

DEER FARMER

Alsheimer, Charles J. *Quality Deer Management: The Basics and Beyond.* Iola, Wisc.: Krause Publications, 2002.

Lee, Leonard. *The Encyclopedia of Deer: Your Guide to the World's Deer Species Including Whitetails, Mule Deer, Caribou, Elk, Moose, and More.* McGregor, Minn.: Voyageur Press, 2004.

Miller, Karl V., and R. Larry Marchinton. *Quality Whitetails: The Why and How of Quality Deer Management.* Mechanicsburg, Pa.: Stackpole Books, 1995.

Von Kerckerinck, Josef. *Deer Farming in North America: The Conquest of a New Frontier.* Rhinebeck, N.Y.: Phanter Press, 1987.

DOWSER

Bird, Christopher. *The Divining Hand: The 500-Year Old Mystery of Dowsing.* West Chester, Pa.: Whitford Press, 2000.

Webster, Richard. *Dowsing for Beginners: The Art of Discovering: Water, Treasure, Gold, Oil, Artifacts*. St. Paul, Minn.: Llewellyn Publications, 1996.

EMU FARMER

Jensen, James M., James H. Johnson, and Stanley T. Weiner. *Husbandry and Medical Management of Ostriches, Emus, and Rheas*. Wildlife & Exotic Animal, 1992.

Minnaar, Maria. *The Emu Farmer's Handbook: Commercial Farming Methods for Emus, Ostriches and Rheas*. Blaine, Wash.: Hancock House Publishing, 1998.

Starkweather, Doug and JoAnna. "Morningstar Ranch." *Emu Today & Tomorrow*. Available online at http://www.emutoday.com/feature.htm.

Tully, Thomas, and Simon M. Shane. *Ratite Management, Medicine, and Surgery*. Melbourne, Fla.: Krieger Publishing, 1996.

FISH FARMER

Landau, Matthew. *Introduction to Aquaculture*. Hoboken, N.J.: John Wiley & Sons, 1991.

Parker, Rick, Ph.D. *Aquaculture Science*. Florence, Ky.: Thomson Delmar Learning, 2000.

FORESTRY CONSULTANT

Beattie, Mollie, Charles Thompson, and Lynn Levine. *Working With Your Woodland: A Landowner's Guide*. Dartmouth, N.H.: University Press of New England, 1993.

Hilts, Stewart. *The Woodland Management Handbook: Making the Most of Your Wooded Property for Conservation, Income or Both*. Richmond Hill, Ontario: Firefly Books, Ltd., 1999.

Vardaman, James M. *How to Make Money Growing Trees*. New York: Wiley, 1989.

GAME BIRD PRODUCER AND HUNT ORGANIZER

Harper, Mavis and Montey. *Raising Game Birds*. North Adams, Mass.: Garden Way Publishing Co., 1984.

Hayes, B. Leland. *Upland Game Birds: Their Breeding and Care*. Leland B. Hayes, 1995.

Scheid, Dan W. *Raising Game Birds*. Brookfield, Wisc.: Lessister Publications, 1986.

GAME WARDEN

Cohen, Paul and Shari. *Careers in Law Enforcement and Security*. New York: The Rosen Publishing Group, Inc., 1995.

Echaore-McDavid, Susan. *Career Opportunities in Law Enforcement, Security, and Protective Services*. New York: Checkmark Books, 2000.

Grosz, Terry. *Wildlife Wars: The Life and Times of a Fish and Game Warden*. Boulder, Colo.: Johnson Books, 1999.

———. *For Love of Wildness: The Journal of a U.S. Game Management Agent*. Boulder, Colo.: Johnson Books, 2000.

Hethcox, Jim. *Adventures in Green & Gray: True Stories of a Game Warden*. Metter, Ga.: Wiregrass Publishers, 2003.

Hodges, Terry. *Tough Customers: True Adventures of Game Wardens and the Outlaws They Pursue*. New York: T & C Books, 1994.

Lee, Mary Price, Richard S. Lee, and Carol Beam. *100 Best Careers in Crime Fighting*. New York: Macmillan, 1998.

Stinchcomb, James. *Opportunities in Law Enforcement and Criminal Justice*. Lincolnwoood, Ill.: NTC./VGM, 1996.

HIKING TRAIL DESIGNER

Birchard, William, Robert D.Proudman, and Michael Dawson. *Appalachian Trail Design, Construction and Maintenance*. Harpers Ferry, W.Va.: Appalachian Trail Conference, 2000.

Birkby, Robert C. *Lightly on the Land: The Trail-Building and Maintenance Manual*. Seattle, Wash.: Mountaineers Books, 1996.

Demrow, Carl, and David Salisbury. *Complete Guide to Trail Building and Maintenance*. Boston: Appalachian Mountain Club Books, 1998.

Flink, Charles A., and Robert M. Searns. *Trails for the Twenty-First Century: Planning, Design, and Management Manual for Multi-Use Trails*. Washington, D.C.: Island Press, 2001.

INSECT CONTROL TECHNICIAN

Bohdan, Michael. *What's Buggin' You?: Michael Bohdan's Guide to Home Pest Control*. Santa Monica, Calif.: Santa Monica Press, 1998.

Fagerlund, Richard. *The Bugman on Bugs: Understanding Household Pests and the Environment*. Albuquerque, N.Mex.: University of New Mexico Press, 2004.

Wilson, Edward O. *For Love of Insects*. Cambridge, Mass.: Belknap Press, 2003.

IRRIGATION SPECIALIST

Keesen, Larry. *The Complete Irrigation Workbook: Design, Installation, Maintenance & Water Management*. Cleveland, Ohio: Franzak & Foster, 1995.

Melby, Pete. *Simplified Irrigation Design*. New York: Wiley, 1995.

Smith, Stephen W. *Landscape Irrigation: Design and Management*. New York: Wiley, 1996.

Tulleners, Robin. *21 Secrets For Irrigation Contractors*. Maple Grove, Minn.: Contrex, 1996.

LANDSCAPE DESIGNER

Beattie, Mollie, Charles Thompson, and Lynn Levine. *Working With Your Woodland: A Landowner's Guide*. Dartmouth, N.H.: University Press of New England, 1993.

Brabec, Barbara. *Creative Cash: How to Profit From Your Special Artistry, Creativity, Hand Skills, and Related Know-How*. Philadelphia: Three Rivers Press, 1998.

Dell, Owen. *How to Start a Home-Based Landscaping Business*. Guilford, Conn.: Globe Pequot, 2002.

Doyle, Michael E. *Color Drawing: Design Drawing Skills and Techniques for Architects, Landscape Architects, and Interior Designers*. 2nd edition. Hoboken, N.J.: John Wiley and Sons, Inc., 1999.

Lang, Cay. *Taking the Leap: Building a Career as a Visual Artist*. San Francisco: Chronicle Books, 1998.

Reid, Grant W. *From Concept to Form: In Landscape Design*. Hoboken, N.J.: John Wiley & Sons, 1993.

Rogers, Elizabeth Barlow. *Landscape Design: A Cultural and Architectural*

History. New York: Harry N. Abrams, Inc., 2001.

MAPLE SYRUP PRODUCER

Beattie, Mollie, Charles Thompson, and Lynn Levine. *Working With Your Woodland: A Landowner's Guide.* Dartmouth, N.H.: University Press of New England, 1993.

Gagnon, John. *Hard Maple, Hard Work.* Marquette, Mich.: Northern Michigan University Press, 1996.

Scardena, David E., ed. *North American Maple Syrup Producers Manual.* Columbus, Ohio: The Ohio State University, 1996.

MUSHROOM GROWER

Hudler, George W. *Magical Mushrooms, Mischievous Molds.* Princeton, N.J.: Princeton University Press, 2000.

Money, Nicholas P. *Mr. Bloomfield's Orchard: The Mysterious World of Mushrooms, Molds, and Mycologists.* London: Oxford University Press, 2002.

Stamets, Paul. *Mushroom Cultivator: A Practical Guide to Growing Mushrooms at Home.* Agarikon Press, 1983.

ORCHARD OPERATOR

Bird, Richard. *Growing Tree Fruit: A Directory of Varieties and How to Cultivate Them Successfully.* Dayton, Ohio: Lorenz Books, 2003.

Otto, Stella. *The Backyard Orchardist: A Complete Guide to Growing Fruit Trees in the Home Garden.* Fort Collins, Colo.: Ottographics, 1995.

Somerville, Warren. *Pruning and Training Fruit Trees.* Cambridge, Mass.: Butterworth-Heinemann, 1997.

Southwick, Larry. *Grafting Fruit Trees.* North Adams, Mass.: Storey Books, 1981.

Stremple, Barbara Ferguson. *All About Growing Fruits, Berries, and Nuts.* Marysville, Ohio: Ortho Books, 1987.

Teskey, Benjamin J. E. *Tree Fruit Production.* New York: Van Nostrand Reinhold, 1988.

Wampler, Ralph, and James E. Motes. *Pick-Your-Own Farming: Cash Crops for Small Acreages.* Norman, Okla.: University of Oklahoma Press, 1984.

ORGANIC FARM MANAGER

Schwenke, Karl. *Successful Small-Scale Farming: An Organic Approach.* North Adams, Mass.: Storey Books, 1991.

OYSTER SHUCKER

Gordon, David G. *Heaven on the Half Shell: The Story of the Northwest's Love Affair with the Oyster.* Portland, Ore.: Westwinds Press, 2001.

PARK RANGER

Bryant, Jennifer, and Pamela Brown. *Zoe McCully: Park Ranger.* Breckenridge, Colo.: Twenty First Century Books, 1991.

Burby, Liza N. *A Day in the Life of a Park Ranger.* New York: PowerKids Press, 1999.

Costain, Meredith. *Park Rangers: Focus, Careers.* Minneapolis, Minn.: Rebound by Sagebrush, 2001.

Farabee, Charles R. *National Park Ranger: An American Icon.* New York: Roberts Rinehart Publishers, 2003.

————. *Death, Daring and Disaster: Search and Rescue in the National Parks.* New York: Roberts Rinehart Publishers, 1998.

Muleady-Mecham, Nancy Eileen. *Park Ranger: True Stories from a Ranger's Career in America's National Parks.* Flagstaff, Ariz.: Vishnu Temple Press, 2004.

Rudman, Jack. *Ranger in the U.S. Park Service.* Syosset, N.Y.: National Learning Corp., 1980.

Webb, Melody. *A Woman in the Great Outdoors: Adventures in the National Park Service.* Albuquerque, N.Mex.: University of New Mexico Press, 2003.

RANGE MANAGER

Bedell, Thomas. *Range management—transactions with federal land managers.* Corvallis, Ore.: Oregon State University Extension Service, 1980.

Driscoll, Richard S. *Managing public rangelands: Effective livestock grazing practices and systems for national forests and national grasslands (U.S. Dept. of Agriculture. AIB-315).* Washington, D.C.: U.S. Forest Service, 1969.

Jones, Andrea L. *Managing small grasslands including conservation lands, corporate headquarters, recreation fields, and small landfills for grassland birds.* Washington, D.C.: U.S. Fish and Wildlife Service, 1997.

U.S. Department of Defense. *Managing natural resources: productive forests, croplands, grasslands, and wetlands rich with wildlife and scenic beauty on U.S. Army lands (SuDoc D 103.2:M 31/2).* Washington, D.C.: Dept. of the Army, 1991.

TIMBER HARVESTER

Andrews, Ralph W. *This Was Logging.* Atglen, Pa.: Schiffer Publishing, 1997.

Beattie, Mollie, Charles Thompson, and Lynn Levine. *Working With Your Woodland: A Landowner's Guide.* Dartmouth, N.H.: University Press of New England, 1993.

Hilts, Stewart, and Peter Mitchell. *The Woodlot Management Handbook: Making the Most of Your Wooded Property for Conservation, Income or Both.* Richmond Hill, Ontario: Firefly Books Ltd, 1999.

Pike, Robert E. *Tall Trees, Tough Men: A Vivid, Anecdotal History of Logging and Log-Driving in New England.* New York: W.W. Norton & Co., 1999.

Vardaman, James M. *How to Make Money Growing Trees.* New York: Wiley, 1989.

TOPIARY GARDENER

Clark, Ethne. *English Topiary Gardens.* New York: Clarkson N. Potter, Inc., 1988.

Clevely, A. M. *Topiary: The Art of Clipping Trees and Ornamental Hedges.* Topsfield, Mass.: Salem House Publishers, 1988.

Curtis, Charles H., and W. Gibson. *The Book of Topiary.* Rutland, Vt.: Charles E. Tuttle Co., Inc., 1985.

Gallup, Barbara, and Deborah Reich. *The Complete Book of Topiary.* New York: Workman Publishing, 1987.

Hammer, Patricia Riley. *The New Topiary: Imaginative Techniques From Longwood Gardens.* New York: Antique Collector's Club, 1991.

Lacey, Geraldine. *Creating Topiary.* New York: Antique Collector's Club, 1987.

TURF SCIENTIST

Beard, James B. *Turf Management for Golf Courses.* 2nd ed. New York: Wiley & Sons, 2001.

Carrow, R.N., D.V. Waddington, and P.E. Rieke. *Turfgrass Soil Fertility & Chemical Problems: Assessment and Management.* New York: Wiley & Sons, 2002.

Christians, Nick. *Fundamentals of Turfgrass Management.* New York: Wiley & Sons, 2003.

Tani, Toshikazu, and James B. Beard. *Color Atlas of Turfgrass Diseases.* New York: Wiley & Sons, 2002.

White, Charles B. *Turf Managers' Handbook for Golf Course Construction, Renovation, and Grow-In.* New York: Wiley & Sons, 2000.

WINEGROWER (VITICULTURALIST)

Cox, Jeff. *From Vines to Wines: The Complete Guide to Growing Grapes and Making Your Own Wine.* North Adams, Mass.: Storey Books, 1999.

Margalit, Yair. *Winery Technology and Operations Handbook.* San Francisco: Wine Appreciation Guild, 1990.

McGrew, J.R., J. Loenholdt, and T. Zabadal, et. el. *The American Wine Society Presents Growing Wine Grapes.* Ann Arbor, Mich.: G.W. Kent, Inc., 1994.

Rombaugh, Lon. *The Grape Grower: A Guide to Organic Viticulture.* White River Junction, Vt.: Chelsea Green Publishing Company, 2002.

Wagner, Philip. *A Wine-Growers Guide.* San Francisco: Wine Appreciation Guild, 1996.

White, Robert E. *Soils for Fine Wines.* London: Oxford University Press, 2003.

Wilson, James E. *Terroir.* Berkeley, Calif.: University of California Press, 1999.

Winkler, Albert J. *General Viticulture.* Berkeley, Calif.: University of California Press, 1975.

INDEX

Page numbers in **bold** indicate main entries.

A

Abdul, Paula 18
Adelaide, University of 117
Aero-Tech 37
agricultural colleges and universities xiii, 139–145. *See also under specific college or university*
state-by-state guide 139–145
Agricultural Marketing Service 99
agronomist **1–4**, 118
AgrowKnowledge 109
Aguilera, Christina 18
alpaca farmer **5–8**, 118–119, 147
Alpaca Owners and Breeders Association 7, 8
Alpaca Registry 6
American Emu Association 49
American Hiking Society 65
American Society of Agronomy 1, 4
American Society of Dowsers 43
American Society of Farm Managers and Rural Appraisers 87
Animal Kingdom Theme Park 109

apiarists 9–12
Appalachian Trail 65
Appleseed, Johnny 83
Aqua-Manna 51
Arachnophobia (film) 18
Association of Professional Landscape Designers 75
associations, organizations, and Web sites xiii, 118–130. *See also under specific topic*
AT&T 18
Audubon Camp (Wyoming) 19

B

Back Country Emus 47
Beaune, University of 117
beekeeper **9–12**, 119, 147
Blaxton, William 83
boatswain 29
Bordeaux, University of 117
Brand Deer Farm 41
buffalero 13–16
buffalo herder **13–16**, 119–120
bug wrangler **17–20**, 120
Burbank, Luther ix
Bureau of Land Management 101, 102

C

California, University of, Davis 18, 117
Cap'n Zach's Crab House 30

career tests and inventories 137–138
Carter, Jimmy 97
Carver, George Washington ix, 97, 98
Central Park 74
Chapman, John (Johnny Appleseed) 83
Christmas tree grower **21–24**, 120–121
Church, Thomas 74
citrus grower **25–27**, 121
Civil Service 62
colleges and universities. *See* agricultural colleges and universities
Colorado, University of 112
Colorado State University 112
Colorado Trail 65
commercial pilot. *See* cropduster
community supported agriculture (CSA) 87, 88
Continental Divide Trail 65
Cooper, Alice 18
Cooperative Extension Service 139
Copycat (film) 18
Cornell University 9, 117
CPRM. *See* professional rangeland manager (CPRM)
crab fisherman **28–31**, 121–122
boatswain 29
first mate 29

cranberry farmer **32–35**, 122

crop duster **36–38**, 122–123

CSA. *See* community supported agriculture (CSA)

Cypress Gardens 107

D

Decas Cranberries 34

deer farmer **39–42**, 123–124

Denver Broncos 112

Departments of Agriculture (state) 1

Disneyland 107

Disney World. *See* Walt Disney World Resort

Downing, Andrew Jackson 74

dowser **43–45**, 124

Drumlin Farm 88

Duxbury Cranberry Farm 34

E

Eastern Apicultural Society of North America 9

Elizabeth I (queen of England) 43

emu farmer **46–49**, 124

entomologists 17

Epcot Park 108

Exorcist II (film) 18

F

Fanucchi Vineyard 115

farmer. *See* alpaca farmer; cranberry farmer; deer farmer; emu farmer; fish farmer; organic farm manager; peanut farmer

Fighter (film) 18

first mate 29

Fish and Wildlife Service 102

fish farmer **50–52**, 124

Florida, University of, Gainesville 26

Flying Pony Alpaca 6, 7

Food and Agricultural Center for Tomorrow 4

forestry consultant **53–56**, 125

Forest Service. *See* U.S. Forest Service

4-H programs 27, 42, 49, 59, 89, 102

Fresno State 117

G

game bird producer and hunt organizer **57–59**, 125

game warden **60–63**, 125–126

gardener. *See* topiary gardener

general careers in agriculture and nature, readings 146

Georgia Peanut Commission 98

Gladlock 18

Global Positioning System 38

Grand Canyon National Park 93

GrassMaster field 112

Guelph, University of 117

H

Harrison, Benjamin 139

Hatch Act of 1889 139

Heretic, The (film) 18

hiking trail designer **64–66**, 126

Humboldt State University 95

hunt organizer. *See* game bird producer and hunt organizer

I

Idol, Billy 18

insect control technician **67–70**, 126

Institute for Food Technologists 4

Internet safety 131

INVESCO Field 112

irrigation specialist **71–73**, 126

J

James and the Giant Peach (film) 18

J.C. Ehrlich, Inc. 68

Jefferson, Thomas 74

Jurassic Park (film) 18

K

Kennett Square 80, 81

King's Canyon 95

L

landscape designer **74–76**, 126–127

Late Show with David Letterman (TV show) 18

Lava Beds National Monument 95

L.A. Woman (film) 18

Letterman, David 18

Lincoln, Abraham 139

Long Beach State College 18

Longwood Gardens 74, 107
Los Angeles State and County Arboretum 18

M

Magical Gathering topiary garden 107
Magic Kingdom Park 108
M. Albright Training Center 93
maple syrup producer 77–79, 127
Massachusetts, University of 48
Massachusetts Maple Producers Association 78
Master Beekeeper Certificate 9
Maxie's Supper Club and Oyster Bar 92
Mile High Stadium 112
Minnesota Deer Association 41
Modoc Nation 95
Monticello 74
Morrill Acts of 1862 and 1890 139
mushroom grower 80–82, 127

N

Naples Daily News 25
National Bison Refuge 14
National Center for Agriscience and Technology Education 109
National Christmas Tree Association 24
National Geographic 18
National Organic Program 86

National Peanut Board 98
National Resource Conservation Service 101, 102
Naumkeag 74
Nebraska, University of 102
North American Deer Farmers Association 39
North American Maple Syrup Producers Manual 78
North Carolina State University Insect Biological Control Projects 20

O

Occupational Outlook Handbook xi, xii, 136–137
Ocean Spray 34
Olmsted, Frederick Law 74
online career resources xiii, 131–138
  career tests and inventories 137–138
  Internet safety 131
  search engines 131–132
  Web sites, helpful 132–138
orchard operator 83–85, 127–128
organic farm manager 86–89, 128
oyster shucker 90–92, 128

P

park ranger 93–96, 128
peanut farmer 97–99, 128–129

Penn State University 2
Pennsylvania Game Commission Bureau of Law Enforcement 62
Pentagon terrorist attacks 36
personal attributes, generally xii
pest control. *See* insect control technician
Petersheim Brothers 44
Phillips Mushroom Farms 81
pilot. *See* cropduster
Polaroid 18
professional rangeland manager (CPRM) 101

R

Race the Sun (film) 18
range manager **100–102,** 129
Rocky Mountain Regional Turfgrass Association 112
Rocky Mountain Regional Turfgrass Research Foundation 112

S

San Francisco Zoo summer Insect Zoo internship 20
SCORE 76
search engines 131–132
September 11, 2001 terrorist attacks 36
Sierra Club 19
Smith-Lever Act of 1914 139
Society for Range Management 101
Soil Conservation Service 1

South Carolina, University of, in Columbia 68
South Face Farm 78
Spider-Man (film) 19
Spring Brook Century Farms 22
Steele, Fletcher 74
Stellenbosch, University of 117
Stephen T. Mather Training Center 93
Summit County Open Space and Trails 65
Super Bowl 112
Sycamore Hollow Farm 58

T
Texas A&M University 72
timber harvester **103–106**, 129
Tonight Show, The (TV show) 18
topiary gardener **107–110**, 129–130

turf scientist **111–113**, 130

U
"Uncle Matt's Organic" 26
universities. *See* agricultural colleges and universities
U.S. Bureau of Labor Statistics xi, 10, 25, 84
U.S. Coast Guard 30
U.S. Department of Agriculture 1, 87
  Agricultural Marketing Service 99
  National Organic Program 86
U.S. Department of Labor 10
U.S. Department of the Interior
  Bureau of Land Management 101, 102
U.S. Forest Service 95, 101, 102

U.S. Geological Survey 43
U.S. National Park Service 93–95
U.S. Small Business Association 76

V
viticulturist. *See* winegrower

W
Walt Disney World Resort 107–109
Weaver, Sigourney 18
Web sites, helpful 132–138
winegrower **114–117**, 130
Wolf Pine Farm 88
World Trade Center terrorist attacks 36

Y
Yellowstone Park 14